Real life, real answers.

Planning for a financially secure retirement

Real life, real answers.

Planning for a financially secure retirement

by
Jim Jenks &
Brian Zevnik

Houghton Mifflin Company   Boston
1990

For information about permission to reproduce selections from this book, write to
Permissions, Houghton Mifflin Company, 2 Park Street, Boston, Massachusetts
02108.

Library of Congress Catalog Card Number: 89-85914
ISBN: 0-395-51098-8

General editors: Barbara Binswanger, James Charlton, Lee Simmons

Design by Hudson Studio

"Real life, real answers" is a trademark of the John Hancock Mutual Life Insurance
Company.

Printed in the United States of America

10 9 8 7 6 5 4 3 2 1

Although this book is designed to provide accurate and authoritative information in
regard to the subject matter covered, neither the authors and general editors nor the
publisher are engaged in rendering legal, accounting, or other professional service.
If legal advice or other expert assistance is required, the services of a competent
professional should be sought.

Contents

CHAPTER I

Taking charge of your future

W hy plan? Simple. To make sure you get what you want. If you want your actual retirement lifestyle to match that idyllic vision you've conjured up in your mind's eye, then you need a financial plan to get you there.

Why plan? To create a personal sense of control; to enjoy the security of knowing you're prepared. To banish fear of the unknown; to reshape your post-work life to your own design; to develop the best combination for you of leisure pursuits, volunteer efforts, time management, part-time work, travel, etc.

Why plan? Because retirement is rich in promise, but to make sure that promise is kept, you need a strong financial plan to guide you. It is not necessary to become rich in monetary terms, but you do want to be rich in terms of options open to you and not be forced by monetary constraints to take small nibbles out of retirement life. Through careful planning you will be able to enjoy new horizons, new advantages, and new opportunities when you reach those "freedom years."

Why plan? Because retirement is fraught with potential dangers. Inflation chews up savings. Uncertainty swirls around Social Security payments. Health care costs skyrocket. Tax-free investments dwindle.

No one can tell you exactly what to do. You need to plot your own course, and this book will help get you started. First, you will take a financial snapshot to focus on where you are today. Then you will project where you want to be in the future. Then you will lay out the financial plan to get you there.

WHAT IS FINANCIAL PLANNING?

Financial planning means taking an organized approach to managing finances—income and assets—so that you get from financial point A to financial point B. It involves making choices, such as whether to spend or save and whether to buy or sell stocks, bonds, or annuities. Financial planning for retirement aims squarely at providing you with an adequate supply of money and managing the inevitable risks.

Before you can map out plans to get from financial point A to financial point B, you must first locate point A. That means analyzing your present financial condition—assets, income, liabilities.

Establishing financial point B is the second part of financial planning. It involves setting solid objectives and retirement goals:

- ☐ Having annual income of X dollars by age X sufficient to sustain your current standard of living and protect yourself against inflation.
- ☐ Building income for the care of your spouse for life.
- ☐ Creating nest eggs to take care of special desires such as travel, family time, and leisure.

WHEN TO START PLANNING

Keep three fundamental truths in mind:

1. The sooner you begin to plan for retirement, the easier it will be to accomplish your financial objectives.
2. It's never too late to get some kind of plan into gear.
3. Financial planning for your retirement is a continuing process that you can begin right now and continue throughout your retirement years.

The Social Security Administration estimates that the average retiree living on over $20,000 per year gets only 42 percent of that income from Social Security, pensions and other benefits and 58 percent from earnings and investments. Suppose you decide that you want to accumulate $100,000 by retirement to fill the gap between your needs and income from Social Security, savings, and perhaps a company pension. And suppose that you will average an 8 percent return and invest your money at the beginning of each year.

Years to retirement	Annual investment needed at 8 percent to reach $100,000
5	$15,782
10	6,392
15	3,410

INFLATION

Another factor at work, one that has been called the cruelest tax, is inflation. A savings nest egg of $100,000 in cash to supplement other income may seem adequate today, but how will it look in the future?

Years to retirement	Buying power of $100,000 at inflation rates of				
	4%	5%	6%	7%	8%
5	$82,190	$78,350	$74,730	$71,300	$68,060
10	67,560	61,390	55,840	50,830	46,320
15	55,530	48,100	41,730	36,240	31,520

Years to retirement	Amounts needed for equivalent purchasing power of $100,000 at inflation rates of				
	4%	5%	6%	7%	8%
5	$121,670	$127,630	$133,820	$140,260	$146,930
10	148,020	162,890	179,080	196,720	215,890
15	180,090	207,690	239,660	275,900	317,220

Even though Social Security payments are indexed to inflation, you can't take much comfort from that fact. For one thing, Social Security provides only a small part of total income for people who seek a comfortable living style. For another, there are proposals to put caps on how much Social Security can increase each year. Other proposals have gone even further. They seek to eliminate the cost-of-living increases altogether.

Add to inflation a related threat to savings: health care costs. Despite Medicare and catastrophic care coverage, you still need to factor into your financial plans the potential costs of long-term health care not covered by Medicare or other health insurance you may have.

BUILDING A NEST EGG

Everyone wants to retire without substantially reducing their standard of living. Yet the average American's retirement income from Social Security, pensions, and invested savings is, at best, no more than 65 percent to 70 percent of preretirement income. To be sure of a comfortable and secure future, you should shoot for a retirement income as close to your preretirement income level as possible. Building a nest egg is more than just stashing away rainy day money. It is essential to a comfortable retirement.

But what are the secrets to building that nest egg? How can you do it without lowering your current spending level so much that your standard of living suffers? Plan.

Why plan? If you're not convinced that sound planning will lead to a more successful retirement, then you can stop reading now and go try those lottery numbers again. But if you're more concerned than ever about achieving a secure retirement, read on.

CHAPTER II

Creating a financial game plan

The purpose of a plan is to achieve financial or estate planning objectives. A plan is a road map that plots the path to your destination. In your case, that destination is a financially secure retirement. But you may have other, perhaps conflicting, goals as well.

For instance, you may want to leave a substantial estate to your children or grandchildren. With enough money set aside and invested, this goal may not conflict with your retirement objectives. But what if you don't have enough money for both? Then choices will have to be made.

First, establish what you have right now. Then figure out how much you can add to that in the years before you retire. There are some statistics available about what percentage of preretirement incomes average retirees need and how average retirees spend their money. You are not average, but we will look at those figures anyway. They will help you arrive at a rough estimate of what your retirement income needs will be.

Next, figure out the amount and timing of income you may expect from Social Security and company pension programs. The further away from retirement you are, the more difficult it is to establish that figure. The difference between that number and your annual income requirements has to be made up by a nest egg of personal savings and investments. If you eventually want to leave that nest egg to your children, it will have to be large enough to generate interest and dividend income sufficient to make up the difference. If it is not large enough, you are still going to want to make sure that you have a financial plan in place that will ensure adequate income for you and your spouse as long as you are alive.

WHAT YOU HAVE NOW

The first step is to establish as nearly as possible your current net worth. Your net worth is simply the difference between everything you own—your assets—and everything you owe—your liabilities.

The Net Worth Worksheet on page 7 lists the items that make up most people's assets and liabilities. Check it over carefully and make sure nothing is missing. You needn't get everything right down to the last penny. Approximations are good enough. Take your time in reviewing the worksheet.

Your assets

Numbers 1, 2, and 3 on this worksheet are easy. If you have cash on hand, add it to what your bank book says is your current checking balance. Look at your most recent statements to value your savings accounts and money market funds. Figure out how much interest you have earned to date on any certificates of deposit (CDs) and add that number to the face amount. Do not do this unless you are positive you will not have to cash in your CDs prematurely. If that's a possibility, deduct any penalty the bank will charge.

Number 4 is easy, too. Check your last statement from your broker, or use the price quotes in the financial sections of *The Wall Street Journal* or your own newspaper.

Life insurance policies (number 5) include tables of cash values. If you have been reinvesting dividends, the cash values may be much more than the tables show. Call your insurance agent and ask for the exact figure.

If you are sure you are going to collect money owed you (numbers 6 and 7), put it down. If you have doubts, do not.

Number 8 may be your biggest asset. It is hard to establish the true current value of a house before it is actually on the

NET WORTH WORKSHEET

1. Cash on hand	$ _____		1. Accounts payable	$ _____	
2. Checking accounts	$ _____		a. Credit cards	$ _____	
3. Savings accounts	$ _____		b. Medical/dental	$ _____	
	$ _____		c. Other _____	$ _____	
	$ _____		2. Notes payable		
4. Stocks, bonds, securities	$ _____		a. Installment purchases	$ _____	
5. Life insurance (cash value)	$ _____		b. Automobile	$ _____	
6. Accounts receivable (money owed you)	$ _____		c. Bank loans/notes	$ _____	
7. Notes receivable (money owed you by promissory notes)	$ _____		d. Life insurance loans	$ _____	
			3. Taxes due	$ _____	
8. Real estate	$ _____		a. Federal	$ _____	
a. Home	$ _____		b. State	$ _____	
b. Other properties	$ _____		c. Local	$ _____	
9. Vested pension(s) (present value)	$ _____		d. Property	$ _____	
			e. Other _____	$ _____	
10. IRA/HR-10/TSA Company savings plan (401(k),etc.)	$ _____		4. Real estate mortgages		
			a. Home	$ _____	
			b. Other _____	$ _____	
11. Annuities	$ _____		5. Other liabilities (specify) _____	$ _____	
12. Business interests	$ _____		_____	$ _____	
13. Other assets	$ _____		_____	$ _____	
a. Home furnishings	$ _____		_____	$ _____	
b. Hobby/sports equipment	$ _____				
c. Art/antiques	$ _____				
d. Jewelry/furs	$ _____				
e. Autos/boats/RVs	$ _____				
f. Other	$ _____				
TOTAL ASSETS	$ _____		TOTAL LIABILITIES	$ _____	

TOTAL ASSETS — TOTAL LIABILITIES = NET WORTH $ _____

market, but any good local real estate broker can give you an estimate. Advice: Deduct 10 percent to 15 percent from that estimate; brokers are eternally optimistic, especially when appraising a home they may get a chance to list.

For numbers 9 and 10, see the benefits administrator of your company, union, or organization to learn the current values of your vested benefits in pension plans, 401(k), 403(b), profit sharing, and savings plans. You are entitled to an annual update of this information (see Chapter IV for more help).

You should have at least an annual statement of value from whoever is administering your Individual Retirement Account (IRA). Depending on what you have invested your IRA money in, you may also be able to find a current price quote in a newspaper.

Check with your insurance agent on annuities (number 11). Remember: current value.

Whether it is a business of your own or money you have invested in some nonpublicly traded company, you may have a hard time fixing a current value for number 12. Unless someone has recently offered to buy you out, thus establishing a price that could actually be received right now, it is best to be very conservative. Talk to your accountant. Unless he or she has a better idea, value your business interests at no more than 25 percent of what you think they are worth.

Home furnishings (13a), other than antiques, which are worth only what a willing buyer will pay for them, are extremely difficult to value. Do not confuse current value with the replacement value an insurance policy may call for. In terms of establishing your net worth, you might value furnishings at 5 percent of your home's market value.

If you have a valuable collection of stamps or baseball cards (13b), you should have a good handle on its current value. Just be very conservative; use the figure you are positive you could get in cash today from a dealer, not the values listed in the guides. That is probably not much more than 50 percent of what you think the collection is worth.

For numbers 13c and 13d, be careful with appraisals. The

only way to establish a real value is to put things on the market. Ask a furrier what he would give you. Of course it's worth more! But not in terms of establishing your net worth.

Use the Galves *Blue Book* for 13e. It gives wholesale or trade-in auto values. Most libraries, all auto dealers, and your automobile insurance agent have a copy. Boats and RVs are harder to get valid numbers for. Check dealers and classified ads for similar vehicles, and be conservative.

Your liabilities

Number 1 on the worksheet includes all the bills you haven't paid. If you bought a VCR for $500 on your credit card yesterday, do not forget to include that, even though you haven't received the bill yet.

If you can't locate the amortization schedules for any of your loans (number 2), ask the lender for the balances. Some loans have prepayment penalties that you should include even if you do not plan on paying early. You want the actual amounts you would be liable for if you eliminated all debts today.

Past tax bills or mortgage statements will show you real estate taxes (number 3). You or your tax preparer can make an estimate of any current income tax liabilities. If your withholding taxes have been sufficient in the past, you may not have any current tax liability.

For number 4, your last mortgage statement should tell you exactly how much more you owe.

Your net worth

As the worksheet shows, add both columns and subtract your liabilities from your assets to establish your net worth—as of today. By next month, it will be somewhat different. By next year, it may be significantly different.

That's why you must calculate your net worth at least once a year, preferably at the same time each year. Do it on a line-by-line basis. Make certain that whatever assumptions you make in fixing values are consistent year after year.

Comparing assets and liabilities on a line-by-line basis each year will give you a valuable means of judging your progress toward a financially secure retirement. In the first chapter, we spoke about locating financial point A. That's your current net asset figure, a snapshot of your financial status at this given point in time. The series of snapshots you will take, year after year, will tell you whether you are making progress toward achieving financial point B.

If your net worth keeps growing each year at a rate that beats inflation, and is consistent with your retirement goals, your game plan is a winner.

HOW MUCH CAN YOU ADD?

Unless you unexpectedly receive an inheritance, win a lottery, or otherwise strike it rich in a way you cannot plan for, the money you must set aside to make your net worth grow each year has to come from your current income. So the obvious assertion is: You have got to make sure you take in more than goes out. For most of us, that means establishing and living within a family budget.

Maybe you have a budget in place right now, and it is working. Congratulations. You are way ahead of the game. Maybe you have tried budgeting a couple of times and failed. Sorry. You have got to try again. Either use a financial planner or find a good guide to budgeting that you can live with. [Editor's note: *The easy family budget*, another *Real life, real answers* guide, can help.]

Whatever budget plan works for you, it will undoubtedly share certain characteristics with other budget plans. It will require you to keep a daily record of everything you make and spend. Each month, you must transfer those records onto a worksheet something like the one provided on page 12. Because of seasonal differences (Christmas, summer vacations, one-time bonuses, annual insurance premiums), you must do this for a full 12-month period to get an accurate fix on all the money that comes in, and all the ways you find to spend it.

Look at the worksheet carefully. Notice that two kinds of

expenses are suggested: fixed (unavoidable and relatively pre-dictable) and variable (less predictable and/or subject to greater control by you). Notice the last item under fixed expenses: Savings/investments/IRAs. Fixed? Isn't savings and invest-ment money what's left over after you have met all your other expenses? The answer is no. The most successful game plans for retirement have all been built on the principle of paying your-self first. That means making a regular savings and investment program as much a part of your regular fixed monthly expenses as your mortgage payments.

Tough? Yes. Unrealistic? No. Millions of people do it, and it works.

As for tracking all of your expenses, what is most amazing is that nearly everyone who does it seems to stop spending as much as before. Maybe it is only a few dollars a month, saved by taking lunch to the office four days a week instead of eating out, or maybe it is cutting back on a major expense, such as an unnecessary second car. Whatever, nearly everyone can find ways to cut back, especially if the goal is as important as a secure retirement.

How much can you add each year to savings and invest-ments that will make your net worth grow? Only you can decide that. While you are tracking your spending and beginning to establish a good record of income and expenses, though, you can look ahead at what you will need and where it may come from.

HOW MUCH WILL YOU NEED?

The American Association of Retired Persons (AARP) has estimated that most retired couples need 65 percent to 70 per-cent of preretirement income to manage comfortably in the post-working years. Others say 80 percent or higher. It really depends on whether your plans include such expenses as increased travel, entertainment, and restaurants. Your costs might even go up.

Keep in mind that these are averages. They may or may not

MONTHLY INCOME/EXPENSES WORKSHEET

Fixed income		**Fixed expenses**	
Gross salary/wages	$ _____	Rent/mortgage	$ _____
Spouse gross	$ _____	Other property	$ _____
Alimony/child support	$ _____	Utilities	$ _____
Benefit income	$ _____	Withholding taxes	$ _____
Social security	$ _____	Taxes (not withheld)	$ _____
Disability	$ _____	Installment loans	$ _____
Life insurance	$ _____	Personal property/	
Pension/retirement	$ _____	rentals/leases	$ _____
Rents	$ _____	Insurance	
Dividends/interest	$ _____	Life	$ _____
Other sources:		Disability	$ _____
_____	$ _____	Auto	$ _____
_____	$ _____	Health	$ _____
_____	$ _____	Transportation	
		(gas, commuting, etc.)	$ _____
		Education	$ _____
		Child care	$ _____
		Food (average)	$ _____
		Payments to others	$ _____
		Alimony	$ _____
		Maintenance	$ _____
		Other	$ _____
		Savings/investments	$ _____

Variable income		**Variable expenses**	
Commissions	$ _____	Clothing	$ _____
Tips	$ _____	Charge accounts	$ _____
Bonuses	$ _____	Medical/dental	$ _____
Interest/dividends	$ _____	Personal	$ _____
Royalties/residuals	$ _____	Travel/camps	$ _____
Business, farm, trade	$ _____	Recreation	$ _____
Other	$ _____	Entertainment	$ _____
		Contribution/gifts	$ _____
		Household	$ _____
		(furnishings, maintenance)	
		Other	$ _____
Total monthly income	$ _____	Total monthly expenses	$ _____

TOTAL MONTHLY INCOME — TOTAL MONTHLY EXPENSES

= NET MONTHLY INCOME $ _____

PERCENTAGES OF INCOME SPENT IN VARIOUS CATEGORIES

Expense category	Age group 55-64	Age group 65-74
Housing	28%	30%
Food and beverages	16	17
Apparel and services	5	4
Transportation	21	19
Health care	5	9
Personal insurance and pensions	11	5
Other—entertainment, reading, education, contributions, etc.	14	16

represent what is important to you and your lifestyle.

The table provided is based on a U.S. Bureau of Labor Statistics study of how people of different ages spend their money. The differences between preretired and retired people are not as significant as you might think, with the exception of health care costs, which nearly double for the older group, and costs of insurance and pensions, which are cut in half.

Certainly, many preretirement expenses are work-related. You will eliminate the costs of commutation and work-related lunches. Your clothing expenses will probably go way down, along with laundry bills. But other expenses, primarily health care, are likely to rise.

One way to get a fairly accurate fix on your own post-retirement expenses is to look at a year's worth of your current monthly expenses. Put a blank line next to each item and begin to fill in your estimate of what that will cost in retirement.

If you plan on staying in your present home and paying off your mortgage by your retirement date, you can lower your housing costs. You will still have to budget for taxes, insurance, repairs, and maintenance, of course. If you plan to move, you are going to have to know where, how much you will spend for a new house, what the tax and insurance rates are, etc.

Use current costs without worrying about inflation. There is a quick and easy way to adjust your estimates upward.

The remaining chapters in this book will help you estimate such retirement expenses as health care. After reading on, come back to finish the worksheet. Even if you decide to use an arbitrary percentage such as 80 percent of your current income, come up with some estimate of what your annual income needs in retirement will be.

HOW LONG WILL YOU NEED INCOME?

The thing to keep in mind about all life expectancy tables such as the one on page 15 is that averages cannot really be used in making a financial plan. If the average life expectancy of a 65-year-old man is another 14 years, that simply means that half of all men that age will die before 79, but half will live beyond. Certainly it wouldn't be prudent to plan to have all of your money run out in 14 years. On the other hand, few people even today live to be 100. If you have to "spend down," you will have to come to some decision about the time span involved.

HOW MUCH WILL COME FROM SOCIAL SECURITY AND PENSIONS?

The next two chapters help you estimate your Social Security and pension benefits. If you are lucky, total income from those two sources will be fairly close to your estimate of annual income needs. But remember: The average retired couple living on $20,000 or more a year gets only 42 percent of that income from Social Security and benefits.

Where does the rest come from? From net worth: your assets and the interest and dividends you will get from those assets.

HOW BIG MUST YOUR NEST EGG BE?

It depends. If you want to leave a sizable estate to your children or grandchildren, you have to consider your nest egg to be

LIFE EXPECTANCY CHART

Current	Life expectancy/male	Life expectancy/female
50	25.4	29.5
55	21.3	25.3
60	17.5	21.2
65	14.0	17.3
70	11.0	13.7
75	8.3	10.3
80	6.2	7.5
85	4.5	5.2
90	3.2	3.4
95	1.9	1.9

Source: John Hancock Mutual Life Insurance Company

---

untouchable. You cannot spend any of the principal , but must instead live only on the dividends and interest that the principle produces annually. Given inflation, to leave an estate in which purchasing power equals the amount of your nest egg upon retirement, you must also reinvest some portion of the income from it.

Or you can "spend down" your assets. One of the ways people do this is by purchasing an annuity, which is a contract with an insurance company that guarantees you (and your spouse) an income for life. You transfer your assets to the company when you do this; depending on the type of annuity you buy, these assets may no longer be part of your estate.

Or you can use a combination of both methods. Most people who live for a number of years after retirement find it necessary to spend some of their principal.

First, take a look at what you might need if you want to preserve your nest egg. Remember that no one knows what inflation rates will be in the future, and estimates of interest rates and yields on various investments are just as unreliable. This simple table presents one possible scenario.

TO HAVE $10,000 IN ANNUAL INCOME AT 65 (ADJUSTED FOR 5 PERCENT INFLATION)

Age	$10,000 equivalent	Necessary capital needed if 8% yield	Monthly savings to accumulate capital if annual yield is 8%
50	$20,790	$259,875	$770
55	16,289	203,613	1,130
60	12,762	159,525	2,187
65	10,000	125,000	125,000

In this scenario, a 50-year-old person who wants to have the equivalent of $10,000 in annual purchasing power in 15 years ($20,790) must begin saving $770 a month to have the nest egg ($259,875) necessary to produce that income. If you are already 65 and will retire next month, you must put away $125,000 that month to have the necessary nest egg.

INFLATION

To equal the purchasing power of $1,000 in today's dollars, here is what you will need:

			Inflation rate of				
Years	2%	3%	4%	5%	6%	7%	8%
5	$1,104	1,159	1,217	1,276	1,338	1,403	1,469
10	1,219	1,344	1,480	1,629	1,790	1,967	2,159
15	1,346	1,558	1,801	2,079	2,397	2,759	3,172
20	1,486	1,806	2,191	2,653	3,207	3,870	4,661
25	1,641	2,094	2,666	3,386	4,292	5,427	6,848
30	1,811	2,427	3,243	4,322	5,743	7,612	10,063
35	2,000	2,814	3,946	5,516	7,686	10,677	14,785
40	2,208	3,262	4,801	7,040	10,286	14,974	21,725

If you "spend down"...

Annuities are one way to give up assets in return for a guaranteed monthly income. But you can also do it with other investments. Suppose you have a nest egg of $100,000 and it yields a constant 8 percent a year. Depending on how much you withdraw from the investment each month, you might "spend down" $100,000 to $0 this way:

	15 years	25 years	35 years	Nest egg untouched
Withdraw per month	$956	$772	$710	$667

Your money will run out in 35 years if you take out $710 each month. If you take out only $667, you will always have the $100,000. Some annuities allow this option as well.

Inflation and the real rate of return

Here's one piece of good news. During the period you are accumulating your retirement nest egg, you should usually be able to invest your money so that it is earning at least 2 to 3 percent more than the current rate of inflation. That margin, the difference between inflation and what an investor can earn, is called the real return on capital. Except for a volatile, very high inflation period in the mid-1970's when inflation exceeded interest rates, a positive annual real return on capital has remained surprisingly reliable.

The real return on capital is generally considered to be the difference between inflation and the interest rate one is paid when invested in a short-term "risk-free" investment such as one-year Treasury bills. Before 1970, the annual real return on capital generally ranged between one and three percent; after 1980 the annual real return rose sharply and is now back around three to four percent.

The real return on capital does not mean that you can't lose money or that you will never earn less than the rate of inflation. On the contrary, it is easy to lose money, and if your money is locked into a long-term bond at a fixed interest rate, it is always possible that inflation will rise above the interest rate you are receiving. That is why a good retirement investment plan should be diversified over several investments, each with different terms and levels of risk and liquidity.

YOUR GAME PLAN

By now, you know that reading a book—any book—is not going to create a retirement plan for you. This chapter calls for a great deal of work on your part. Even if you decide to get expert help from a financial planner or other adviser, you are the only one who will be able to make the most important choices and decisions.

Using a financial planner makes a great deal of sense for many people. But you must understand every step of the process used to create your own financial game plan. It doesn't make sense to pay expensive experts to figure out items on a net asset worksheet or a monthly income/expenses worksheet that you can do yourself.

Even if you use an adviser, try to work out a rough game plan of your own. You will save a lot of time and money when the adviser reviews what you have done, and you will have a much better understanding of the issues to be resolved.

Here's a checklist for your review.

1. Establish your net worth and update your net worth worksheet at least once a year on a line-by-line basis.
2. Take control of your income and expenses. Budget for regular savings as a fixed expense, paying yourself first.
3. Estimate your post-retirement expenses.
4. Estimate your Social Security and pension benefits.
5. Calculate the difference between (3) and (4) and decide how large your nest egg of investments should be when you retire.
6. Make adjustments for inflation.
7. Review any plan you make at least once each year.

CHAPTER III

Getting a handle on retirement income: Social Security

T oo many people look at Social Security as the financial cushion for their old age. It's not. View it more as one leg of a three-legged stool on which your retirement seat will rest along with private pensions and personal investments.

Social Security is forever changing. Benefits get changed. Tax bases get increased. Percentage of income taxed goes up. Cost of living adjustments (COLAs) get calculated each year based on the Consumer Price Index, which is forever fluctuating. So any estimate of future Social Security payments is just that—an estimate.

You can take advantage of Social Security in various ways. Retire "early" and choose a lower stipend. Retire "on time" and get a normal amount. Retire "late" and get bigger bucks. Other elements of Social Security, such as spousal payments and disability, can increase benefits.

Understand that Social Security retirement benefits are individualized. They depend on your personal work history: how many years you worked, how much you earned each year, at what age you decide to retire, and how you decide to tap your portion of the Social Security cash outflow.

HOW DOES THE MONEY GO IN?

Social Security is a partnership. You and your employer pay in.

The government decides how much. In 1989 the price tag to you was 7.51 percent of your wages up to a federally decided cap of $48,000. Your share of the tax is withheld by your employer, who then combines it with his equal share and sends it to the Social Security Administration (SSA). That combined share was 15.02 percent of your under-cap 1989 wages.

If you made $25,000, you paid $1,877.50. If you made $48,000 or more, you paid a maximum of $3,604.80. In 1990 the percentage is 7.65 percent and the cap exceeds $50,000. The SSA advises that the percentage of wages taxed may rise to a 10.15 percent individual rate by the year 2020.

WHEN DOES THE MONEY COME OUT?

You may retire at age 65 with full benefits or at 62 with reduced benefits. The age for full benefits is scheduled to rise gradually until it becomes 67. Right now, at 62, your benefits will be 80 percent of what you would have received if you were 65. At 63, they will be 86.5 percent and at 64, about 93.3 percent. Whatever age you choose for early retirement, your benefits will continue to be calculated on that base figure throughout your retirement years, though the COLAs will boost them a trifle each year.

If you continue to work for wages past age 65, your benefits when you do retire increase 3 percent for each year worked up to age 70. Suppose you could retire at age 65 with a monthly income of $490, but you continued working another year; your benefits when you retired at 66 would be $504.70 a month. If you worked until you were 67, you would retire with $519.40 a month. The benefits for additional work years will rise gradually so that by 2000, each year worked beyond 65 will increase benefits by 8 percent. At age 70, the benefits of delaying retirement stop; there is no difference between retiring at 70 or retiring at 75.

HOW MUCH MONEY WILL YOU RECEIVE?

The amount you can expect will be based on what you and your

SOCIAL SECURITY ADMINISTRATION

Request for Earnings and Benefit Estimate Statement

To receive a free statement of your earnings covered by Social Security and your estimated future benefits, all you need to do is fill out this form. Please print or type your answers. When you have completed the form, fold it and mail it to us.

1. Name shown on your Social Security card:

First ⬜ Middle Initial ⬜ Last

2. Your Social Security number as shown on your card:

⬜⬜⬜ - ⬜⬜ - ⬜⬜⬜⬜

3. Your date of birth: Month ⬜⬜ Day ⬜⬜ Year ⬜⬜

4. Other Social Security numbers you may have used:

⬜⬜⬜ - ⬜⬜ - ⬜⬜⬜⬜
⬜⬜⬜ - ⬜⬜ - ⬜⬜⬜⬜

5. Your Sex: ⬜ Male ⬜ Female

6. Other names you have used (including a maiden name):

_____

7. Show your actual earnings for last year and your estimated earnings for this year. Include only wages and/or net self-employment income subject to Social Security tax.

A. Last year's actual earnings:

$ ⬜⬜⬜ , ⬜⬜⬜ . 0 0
Dollars only

B. This year's estimated earnings:

$ ⬜⬜⬜ , ⬜⬜⬜ . 0 0
Dollars only

8. Show the age at which you plan to retire: _____

Form SSA-7004-PC-OP2 (6/88) DESTROY PRIOR EDITIONS

9. Below, show an amount which you think best represents your future average yearly earnings between now and when you plan to retire. The amount should be a yearly average, not your total future lifetime earnings. Only show earnings subject to Social Security tax.

Most people should enter the same amount as this year's estimated earnings (the amount shown in 7B). The reason for this is that we will show your retirement benefit estimate in today's dollars, but adjusted to account for average wage growth in the national economy.

However, if you expect to earn significantly more or less in the future than what you currently earn because of promotions, a job change, part-time work, or an absence from the work force, enter the amount in today's dollars that will most closely reflect your future average yearly earnings. Do not add in cost-of-living, performance, or scheduled pay increases or bonuses.

Your future average yearly earnings:

$ ⬜⬜⬜ , ⬜⬜⬜ . 0 0
Dollars only

10. Address where you want us to send the statement:

Name _____

Street Address (Include Apt. No.; P.O. Box, or Rural Route) _____

City _____ State _____ Zip Code _____

I am asking for information about my own Social Security record or the record of a person I am authorized to represent. I understand that if I deliberately request information under false pretenses I may be guilty of a federal crime and could be fined and/or imprisoned. I authorize you to send the statement of my earnings and benefit estimates to me or my representative through a contractor.

Please sign your name (Do not print)

_____

Date _____ (Area Code) Daytime Telephone No. _____

SP ⬜

21

employer have contributed. Your "account" has been kept by the Social Security Administration over the years, no matter how many gaps in employment you have had or how many different employers.

In fact, you should check with the SSA every two or three years to make sure it has correct records of your contributions, especially if you have changed jobs. Keep evidence of your earnings until you are sure you have received appropriate credit. If the SSA has not credited your account properly, you may be out of luck after three years have gone by unless you have such proof.

You can get the facts and figures for your personal account in two ways. If you are between 60 and 65, call your local SSA office and ask the Teleclaim computer service for the amount you have paid in, the number of quarters you have been credited with, and estimates of what you should be eligible to receive if you retire at 62, 65, or later.

At any age, you can call (800) 937-2000 and get form SSA-7004, the Request for Earnings and Benefit Estimate Statement (REBES) (see sample on page 21).

An estimate

When you fill out the REBES, you will have to estimate future average yearly earnings and project the age at which you plan to retire. The instructions tell you to show an amount that represents your best estimate of annual income (not total lifetime income). Many people use the number for the current year. This saves a lot of headaches.

If you want a closer guesstimate, look into your personal crystal ball. Will you stay in the same job until you retire? Is a big promotion or job switch on the horizon? Will you stop earning taxable income for a period before you start collecting Social Security?

Send the form to the SSA and a few weeks later they will send you the following:

☐ An account of how much of your salary has been taxed each year for Social Security. If your earnings are wrong, or if you see a blank where earnings should have been, call the SSA immediately.

☐ Information on how many "work credits" you need to qualify for Social Security's various programs and whether you have hit the magic number. For the SSA's retirement payments, for example, you must meet a "quarters of coverage" requirement, which depends on your date of birth. For each quarter of a year in which you paid Social Security taxes on a minimum of $500, you get credit for one quarter. In 1989 you needed 40 quarters to qualify.

☐ Your estimated monthly retirement benefits, assuming that you quit work at one of three ages: the age you put down on the REBES form; the full retirement age (anywhere from 65 to 67, depending on how old you are); or age 70.

☐ The monthly benefit your spouse and children could get if you died or became totally disabled.

OPTIONS AND EXEMPTIONS

If both spouses have worked, they have the choice of taking their individual retirement benefits or a couple's share (covered spouse plus half), whichever is larger. Age is a factor here, too. To get the couple benefit, the spouse must be exactly the same age or older than the Social Security recipient. If the spouse is younger, the second part (one half) of the couple's share is reduced.

Suppose your benefit is $790 and your spouse's is $350. You would be better off not claiming your spouse's benefits but instead taking $790 plus half ($395), the couple's calculation, assuming the "better half" is the same age or older.

Widows and widowers who are collecting a deceased spouse's Social Security benefits should bide their time before entering into another marriage. Benefits may stop if you remarry before age 60. After age 60, you can generally collect benefits from either your late spouse or your new one, whichever amount is greater.

There is also an exempt limit on post-retirement income

(which like all of Social Security is subject to change). That means you can earn money up to a certain point, but when you go over that point, you start losing part of your Social Security income. Those who collected early retirement checks (62 to 64) before 1990 lost $1 of Social Security income for every $2 they earned over $6,480 (estimate for 1990: $6,840). To pick an easy amount for calculation, say they earned $8,480 or $2,000 over the exempt limit. They lost $1,000 in benefits.

The exempt limit for 65 to 69-year-old Social Security collectors was $8,880 in 1989 (estimate for 1990: $9,360). If they made $10,880 in income, they lost $1,000 in Social Security payments. In 1990 and beyond, the 65 to 69 group loses $1 of Social Security benefits for every $3 they take in over the exempt amount (the 62 to 64 group stays at $1 for every $2). If you make enough money, you will wind up giving all your Social Security dollars back to Uncle Sam.

If you are over 70 and still going strong on the income scene, you can forget all the calculations. There is no limit to what you can earn starting the month you turn 70.

THE QUESTION OF AGE

While it's true you can start getting a piece of the Social Security pie when you hit 62, you may not want to retire then. Not only are your early retirement benefits lower, but so are those of your spouse. If you opt for checks at 62, that extra one half of your check that your spouse is entitled to drops 25 percent ($16^{2}/_{3}$ percent at 63 and $8^{1}/_{3}$ percent at 64).

The SSA has added financial benefits to make waiting past 65 attractive. The annual extra percentage you get for waiting increases gradually until it reaches 8 percent in the twenty-first century. So if you hold off until after you are 65, the base on which you draw gets bigger and bigger.

There's an argument, however, for the early retirement decision. Say you would be eligible to retire at 65 on $800 per month. That means only $640 at 62. But that would mean 36 payments of $640 before you ever reach 65. Over $23,000. It would take 12 years of the higher payments after regular retirement age to make up the spread.

At the same time, keep in mind the magic 65 number for retirement is creeping higher. Starting at the turn of the century, it will notch up until it hits 66 in 2009 and 67 in 2027. Reduced payments will still be available for early retirement (62), but the reduction will be even steeper.

Another consideration: If you apply for early benefits while you are 62 to 64, you start getting payments in the month you apply. If you apply late for early benefits, you could miss some. If you apply late after you are 65, you can get up to six months' worth of checks retroactively.

APPLYING FOR BENEFITS

As you get closer to your retirement age, you will need to know more about the nuts and bolts of applying for your benefit package. Here are a few points to keep in mind:

1. Plan ahead. Do not wait until the month you retire to head for your local SSA office to get all the forms. In fact, you can apply up to three months before you want (or are entitled to) benefits.
2. Benefits are generally payable only for months in which you are eligible through the entire month. If you are 65 on August 13, benefits start in September.
3. You will need your Social Security card or a record of it; proof of age, such as birth or baptismal certificate, school record, or draft card; a W-2 form for the last two years you worked or a copy of your federal income tax return if self-employed. You can fill out all the papers for your spouse, take them home for him or her to sign, and return them to the SSA office. This saves one of you an office visit.
4. If you retire in the middle of a year, you get your first Social Security retirement check at the end of the first month after you retire.
5. You can get your benefit deposited electronically in your bank account by filling in a form that your bank will file for you.

6. When you retire after being self-employed, expect more questions and proofs required than if you retired after being in someone else's employ. The SSA is always concerned that the self-employed may continue to draw earnings from their businesses while claiming to be retired.

CHAPTER IV

Private pension plans: paving the road to retirement security

I t is important to check the status of your Social Security account. It is equally important to find out where you stand with your current employer's or union's pension plan. If you were covered in previous jobs, check your status in those plans, too. For many people, pension plans produce the single largest source of income for retirement—larger than that of Social Security, savings, or even the two combined. Most plans fall into one of the following types.

A defined benefit plan says that when you meet certain requirements as to age and length of service, it will pay you a definite sum of money, a defined benefit, starting at some future date. You could get X dollars a month for the rest of your life. Or you could get a lump sum calculated by actuaries to be the amount, if invested, that would buy for you monthly payments of X dollars for your lifetime.

A defined contribution plan, sometimes called a money purchase plan or profit sharing plan, says that your employer will set aside some specific sum (or percentage of your pay) each year in an account earmarked for you. You may, in some cases, be allowed to add money of your own. That money will be invested to increase its value along the way. As with the defined benefit plan, you can turn money in your account into a plan that makes monthly payments to you. Or you can sweep your account clean and take out all the cash that has been built up.

The defined benefit plan backed by the employer guarantees a specific monthly income when you retire. The defined contribution plan, however, guarantees only that you will get the employer's contributions plus the earnings. It does not say how much money that will be, how much interest will be earned, or how much your monthly lifetime payments will be when you retire.

Many companies set up profit sharing plans, a form of defined contribution plan, to give their employees retirement income. Contributions to these plans vary each year depending on profits or management's inclination.

With a profit sharing type pension plan, companies can stop contributing when there are low or no profits. Or they can make contributions geared to profits. They cannot, however, indefinitely omit sharing some profits or the plans will lose their tax advantages. Usually profit sharing plans provide less certainty and less money for retirement than do defined benefit and defined contribution plans. They do not provide a defined benefit.

Some defined benefit plans provide for integration of the private pension benefit with the amount you will get from Social Security. Suppose your company's plan would provide you with a monthly payment upon retirement of $1,200. At the same time, say you would be eligible for $600 a month from Social Security. An integrated plan calls for an offset, that is, a subtraction of some percentage of the Social Security amount from the benefit you would otherwise receive from the employer plan. Suppose the plan calls for an offset of 50 percent of the Social Security amount. You would lose 50 percent of the $600 Social Security amount, or $300, from your monthly payment from the plan. You would then get $900 from the private plan and $600 from Social Security for a total of $1,500 a month.

HOW MUCH CAN YOU COUNT ON?

The administrators of qualified plans must furnish certain information to every participant and retiree. Upon written request, the administrator must give you a statement of the total benefits you have accrued.

Among the required items you must be given is a summary plan description (SPD). If you do not have one, ask for a copy and keep it. The SPD should give you enough information so that you can estimate your monthly benefit after retirement.

One company includes a chart in its SPD of its defined benefit plan. Participants can use this to estimate their monthly pensions. Here's what it looks like for someone making $36,000 a year after 30 years of coverage in the company's pension plan.

HOW TO ESTIMATE MONTHLY RETIREMENT INCOME AT NORMAL RETIREMENT DATE

1. Estimate your final average monthly compensation.	$ 3,000
2. Take 1.3 percent of that estimated compensation.	$ 39
3. Enter your number of years of credited service.	30
4. Multiply line 2 by line 3 to get your estimated monthly retirement payment under the plan.	$ 1,170
5. Estimate your primary Social Security benefit.	$ 600
6. Add lines 4 and 5 to obtain your estimated total monthly retirement income.	$ 1,770

(Note item 2 in the above list. This percentage varies from company to company. You should be able to find yours in the SPD if you use this form to estimate your pension.)

VESTING

Although you accrue retirement benefits while participating in a defined benefit, defined contribution, or profit sharing pension plan, you do not have a right to these benefits unless they are vested. Vesting means that if you work for a minimum period that is specified in the pension plan, you are assured of at least some pension or lump-sum payment at retirement.

Some plans require or allow contributions from employees. These gain in value from interest paid on them, as do the employer's contributions. Those benefits that derive from the participant's own contributions are immediately and fully vested.

The law requires that if you are a participant in a plan, and make a request in writing, the administrator of each qualified plan must give you a statement of the total benefits you have accrued, the amount (if any) vested, or the earliest date on which accrued benefits will become vested.

Your vesting rights

How much value or vested benefit you have built up depends on the number of years you have participated in the plan, not the number of years you have worked. This is particularly important for people who may have worked for 30 or 40 years for several employers, but have participated in individual company plans for fewer years.

Even though you have accrued certain benefits from participating in a plan, you have a right to the employer's contribution only for the amount that has become vested. Vesting gives you the legal right to get your benefits at retirement.

In general, plans choose one of two types of vesting: (1) "cliff" or 100 percent vesting for participation for five years; or (2) "graded vesting," 20 percent vesting after three years and another 20 percent each year until 100 percent vesting after seven years. Examine your SPD to find out which method your plan uses. Some multiemployer (usually union) plans have somewhat different schedules that have been reached through collective bargaining.

OPTIONS

Do not put off planning how to take your pension benefit until the last minute. If you understand the options now, you will not be hit by the unexpected when you get to the human resources office.

Real life, real answers.

H arry Batchelder was mapping out his retirement strategy. Corporate planning was his forte, since that had been one of his main functions at Chicago-based Allica Services, Inc. for almost four decades. Now, just months from retirement, his decisions and choices were being made on a much more personal level.

He was all set for Social Security, ready to begin collecting right after the end of the year when he retired and almost simultaneously hit his sixty-fifth birthday. He had already been to the Social Security office and knew his payments from that source and just when they would start.

Now he wanted the same questions answered for his company pension: How much could he expect each month and when would it start? He had been a member of a defined benefit plan at Allica for the last 31 years.

Harry had his summary plan description and had seen the chart for figuring out monthly payments. Now he plugged in his income figures and the number of years he had worked and came out with an estimate.

Then he read that he could get a payout option that would provide survivor benefits for his wife. It would cut a slice from his monthly check during his lifetime, but it would pay her 50 percent of his pension if he died before she did. This appealed to Harry for a number of reasons.

First of all, Harry's wife, Sue, was eight years his junior. Secondly, while Harry had been enjoying good health the last few years, he had undergone heart bypass surgery six years ago. Without being gloomy about it, he figured the odds were pretty high that Sue would outlive him. Lastly, the Batchelders weren't overly concerned by lower monthly checks. Sue was working part-time and Harry planned to convert a lifelong woodworking hobby into a source of income. A local shop had agreed to sell his hand-carved decoys and handcrafted fishing rods; he expected to earn from $5,000 to $8,000 a year from this.

Harry and Sue agreed that the advantages of the survivor's benefit option far outweighed the disadvantages.

Many pension plans, whether defined benefit, defined contribution, or profit sharing, give participants several options from which to choose. They can, for example, choose what is known as "term certain" payments. These payments are for a fixed amount and are guaranteed for 10 years, whether or not the participant lives 10 years. The payments will continue beyond the guaranteed 10 years for participants' full lifetimes. These "term certain" payments are smaller than those that would be paid just for the life of the participant.

Some plans have an option that allows a participant to take a smaller amount than he or she would get for life if taken for his or her life alone, with the spouse getting the exact same amount for life even if the participant dies. Many plans let the participant elect to receive a lump sum that has been actuarially calculated to be equal in value to the monthly payments to be received for life.

The amounts vary by option because of the guarantees of coverage. The law, though, requires that if the prospective pensioner is going to take the monthly payment for his or her lifetime only, the spouse must consent to that option in writing. Some other elections also require consent. Your plan administrator should spell them out. To make a good decision you need to ask for exact money figures for each option.

TAXES

If you take a lump-sum cash pension payment all at once, you trigger what is known as a "taxable event." If you retire and take it before age $59^1/2$, you will not only get clobbered with ordinary income tax on your lump-sum cash, but also with a 10 percent penalty. But at any age, you will have several ways to cushion the tax liability, at least temporarily.

You can, of course, accept the lump sum and pay ordinary income tax on it. Depending on which state you live in and its tax rates, you could pay as much as one-third of the lump-sum total in taxes. Not that you will not pay tax on monthly payments— they just spread out the tax over the rest of your life.

If you were born before January 1, 1936, you may be able to have the portion of the pension distribution that is attributable to your participation in the plan before 1974 (if any) taxed as a long-term capital gain.

The remainder will be taxed as ordinary income, or under five-year or, if you are eligible, ten-year averaging rules that may reduce your taxes. If you are eligible for both, you should have a competent tax professional work out the averaging for both five- and ten-year alternatives and pick the one most favorable to you.

Partial escape

You can temporarily escape paying any taxes by taking the cash from your company plan and putting it into a new qualified plan or an IRA within 60 days after receipt of the money. This process is called "rolling over a lump sum." You can also roll over part of the cash and use the rest for whatever you like. The partial rollover will be tax-deferred until you are age $70^1/2$ or until you start pulling cash out. You will pay tax on the rest. The cash you take, though, will not be eligible for five- or ten-year averaging.

OTHER EMPLOYER PLANS

Two of the best deals to help provide employees with income for retirement are known by a familiar combination of numerals and letters, 401(k) and 403 (b). The 401(k) plans are for profit-making corporations and the 403 (b) for nonprofit organizations, educational institutions and the like. They are similar, except that the 403 (b) allows a little higher annual contribution. Only the 401 (k) will be discussed here.

The 401(k) has been given various monikers: pension plan, thrift plan, profit sharing plan, and salary reduction plan. It has characteristics of a pension plan and a profit sharing plan and has become popular for a variety of reasons. You can use a 401(k) to save on annual personal income tax, to shelter from any tax the earnings in the fund, to get matching contributions from your employer, and, possibly, to obtain loans for "hardships" that may include medical and educational expenses. All in all, you should participate in a 401(k) plan if you are lucky enough to work for a company that offers one.

You will get an annual statement from the company that shows just how much money you have credited to you in the 401(k). You will have options on how to take the accumulations in your account when you retire, somewhat the same as with the distributions from a defined pension plan. In most 401(k)s, you will also have options as to how the money is invested.

If you retire before you are $59^1/2$, though, you will be subject to the 10 percent penalty tax if you withdraw funds from your 401(k). You can, of course, roll over a lump sum distribution into an IRA or another qualified plan before you are $59^1/2$ and defer taxation. Some companies even allow ex-employees to keep the money for a period of time in their accounts in the company's 401(k).

EMPLOYEE STOCK OWNERSHIP PLANS (ESOPS)

ESOPs are classified as pension plans. Do not confuse them with various kinds of stock purchase or stock option plans. Many people think the "O" in ESOP stands for "option." Not so, it stands for "ownership." ESOPs are also known as stock bonus plans. They cost you nothing and have the potential to be worth a lot.

The primary difference between ESOPs and most pension plans is that ESOP assets are generally in the stock of your employer. These company stock assets are "allocated" to you and other eligible participants in the plan. You acquire vested rights to them in much the same way as in defined benefit plans.

When you retire, many plans require that the stock allocated to you be offered to the corporation first. If it refuses to buy the shares at fair market value, you receive them and either keep or sell them. You face the same decisions regarding what to do with the values you have received, whether in stock or cash, as you do with lump-sum payments from other plans.

INDIVIDUAL RETIREMENT ACCOUNTS (IRAs)

If you do not have an IRA (Individual Retirement Account), you are missing a good bet for deferring taxes on earnings that can build up for your retirement.

Many individuals do not open IRAs because they think they must contribute $2,000 each and every year. Not true. After opening an account for as little as $250, you can contribute as little each year as you want (even zero). However, you cannot put in more than $2,000 for yourself and $250 for a nonworking spouse in a year. A working spouse, though, can contribute as much as $2,000 per year.

Other people think they cannot take a tax deduction for their contribution because their earnings are too high and they are participants in a company pension plan. This is not necessarily true either. As of 1989 IRA contributions are still tax-deductible for couples with adjusted gross incomes (AGIs) under $40,000 and partially deductible for AGIs between $40,000 and $50,000. For single persons, the AGI limits are $25,000 to $35,000.

The IRS administers IRAs. For a copy of an informative booklet about IRAs write to Pension Benefit Guaranty Corporation, Coverage and Inquiries Branch (2020 K Street N.W., Washington, DC 20006).

Withdrawals from IRAs before age $59^{1/2}$ are subject to the ubiquitous 10 percent penalty tax. Payments from them must start by age $70^{1/2}$ with minimum withdrawals mandated in accordance with calculations taken from a schedule conveniently published each year in IRS Publication 590. Cash withdrawn is subject to ordinary income tax. You can continue to contribute to IRAs until age $70^{1/2}$, but thereafter fund flows are a one-way street—out.

KEOGH PLANS (HR-10s)

HR-10s are more commonly known as Keogh plans. Designed for people who are self-employed, they have higher tax-deductible amounts than IRAs, and the amounts must be a percentage of self-employment earnings. If you earn only $2,000, you can put it all into an IRA. Not so with the Keogh: only up to 25 percent of the $2,000 would be allowed. The maximum annual amount allowed as a contribution to a Keogh is $30,000. Setting up a Keogh is much more complicated than setting up an IRA, but well worth the trouble. Make sure you use a tax professional. You can have both a Keogh and an IRA.

SIMPLIFIED EMPLOYEE PENSION PLANS (SEPs)

SEPs, simplified employee pension plans, allow employers to contribute to employees' Individual Retirement Accounts. You can have your employer make contributions on your behalf to your IRA. They are limited to 15 percent of your annual earnings to a maximum of $30,000. You can contribute part of your earnings to the SEP under terms similar to those of salary reduction plans such as the 401(k).

All these personal pension plans are useful vehicles for building up sources of income for a financially secure retirement. They all have tax deferrals, penalties for withdrawals before age 59$\frac{1}{2}$, and the requirement that you start drawing down by age 70$\frac{1}{2}$. The latest tax law requires any type of pension plan to start payments to participants at age 70$\frac{1}{2}$, even to those individuals who continue employment beyond that age.

CHAPTER V

Personal investments

T here are many good books on investing, and this chapter doesn't attempt to cover as much ground as they do. [Editor's note: One book is *How to make basic investment decisions*, another *Real life, real answers* guide.] However, this chapter will focus on general principles of investing to produce income for and during retirement.

Keep in mind that the acquisition of capital (money and property) before retirement is different after retirement. It is much easier to accumulate assets while you are working and have an income stream feeding your capital growth. Post-retirement income comes from pensions, Social Security payments, and dividends and interest from wise investment of your capital.

Almost inevitably, you will find a gap between what you will need to live comfortably during retirement and the income provided by Social Security and pensions. That is where personal savings and investment plans come to the rescue.

One crucial piece of advice: Avoid any investment or investing technique that you do not understand. You do not need to deal with such arcane things as naked options, straps, straddles and other gobbledegook to make money. Easier to understand and safer choices are so numerous that you do not need a translator to find them.

INFLATION

When you go to the track for a day of betting on the ponies, you can always choose to sit out a race or two. But when it comes

Real life, real answers.

Jack and Judy McCormack assumed they had a good game plan. As they approached retirement, they thought they had all their financial ducks lined up. They had no outstanding loans and they were quite satisfied living where they were. Based on that seemingly bright picture, they painted this annual income/expense scenario.

Social Security	$10,000
Private pension	12,000
Income from savings	6,000
Total income	$28,000

Projected expenses for first year of retirement:

Housing	$7,800
Food	4,500
Apparel and services	1,000
Transportation	4,900
Health care	2,400
Personal insurance	1,200
Other (entertainment, taxes, etc.)	4,200
Total expenses	$26,000

That nice surplus of $2,000 in the first year looked good until their accountant made them peer five years down the road. Using a "modest" 4 percent inflation rate, Social Security increased by about $8,500 in five years. But their pension payment was fixed and they planned to put all their savings into fixed-income investments. So their annual income in five years reached $29,700. Housing, other than property taxes and repairs, was fixed at $7,800 a year. Applying the same "modest" 4 percent annual inflation rate for five years to all other expenses, they were horrified to see that their expenses ballooned to $29,964. That's a deficit of $264 in their fifth year. And it gets worse: At age 70, five years after their retirement, the McCormacks' life expectancy may be another 15 years. During each of those years their deficit would grow ever deeper, unless they planned to do something to fight inflation.

to inflation, you are *forced* to play.

It is unfortunate that so many politicians and economists today describe inflation rates of 4 percent to 5 percent as "modest." They conveniently forget that the 1950's and early 1960's had rates of only 1 percent and 2 percent. There is nothing modest about a 5 percent increase if you are planning to live on a fixed income for a number of years.

Remember that the purchasing power of a nest egg of $100,000 at an inflation rate of 4 percent plunges to about $67,500 in 10 years and to $56,500 in 15 years. So-called modest rates simply are not tolerable during retirement.

Many people opt to invest their nest eggs solely in fixed-income securities. Until the last couple of decades, that was the accepted and conservative way to treat retirement money. But is it realistic under persistent inflationary conditions?

HISTORY'S LESSONS

Past performance of investments does not necessarily predict the future, but it does offer useful clues. The following chart compares investment returns over more than 60 years:

Security	Annual investment return (%)
U.S. Treasury bills	3.5
Long-term bonds	4.4
Mix of stocks, bonds, and T bills	6.5
Equities (stocks)	10.0

The above chart is based on the concept of total return on investments. The annual investment returns shown on the chart were produced by the reinvestment of all dividends and interest and by annual compounding. Total returns include both the growth in value of the security and the interest and dividends that it produces. For example, if the price of a stock rises 10 percent in a year and pays a 5 percent dividend, the total return for that year is 15 percent. If a stock's value drops 10 percent and pays a 5 percent dividend, then the total return is minus 5 percent. That concept of total return applies to stocks, bonds, mutual funds, tax-exempt securities.

Don't forget to consider the total return. You can get more than just the cash dividends when you invest in equities. It is an important consideration for increasing your retirement nest egg. When you hold bonds to maturity, you will get back their face value, but no more.

It is clear that equities over time have produced far greater total returns than have fixed-income bonds. Investing for retirement is a long-term proposition. Still, you must consider other factors—risk tolerance, age, and immediate income needs—before selecting your own investment strategy. Be flexible. Do not think that you can just invest and forget. Economic conditions change, just as personal factors such as age, risk tolerance, tax bracket, and income needs change. You must adjust to them.

RISK TOLERANCE

How much risk you are willing to take normally depends upon age, dependents, income, and assets. Taking your risk pulse is a task that you should do at least annually. When you check your net worth each year, consider your feelings about risk. The result of your analysis bears strongly on the investment strategies you should use.

You can get a fix on your attitude toward risk by asking yourself how you feel about the statements below. Do you fully agree, partly agree, or strongly disagree with each of them?

1. I am very concerned that my income will not keep up with inflation.
2. I want maximum total return right now.
3. I want to be able to get out of any investment quickly even if I have to take less money for it.
4. I want maximum growth of my savings from now until retirement.
5. I do not want all my nest eggs in one basket.

6. I want any savings to be invested so that I cannot lose any of the money I have put in.

7. I want my investments to go up more than the market indexes when they are high and to go down less when they are low.

If you agree fully with statements 1, 2, 4, and 7, you should have a fairly high tolerance for risk. You should be willing to take some chances with your savings. That does not mean, though, that you shouldn't hedge your bets and use intelligent investing.

If you agree partly with those same statements, you are not totally against risk. If you disagree strongly with those assertions and agree fully with statements 3 and 6, you want safety above all else.

THE AGE FACTOR

For discussion purposes here, investments are categorized as no risk, low risk, and higher risk. There are also high risk and speculative investments, but they have no place in retirement planning. Books on investing give more complete explanations of risks by type of investment. In general, though, U.S. Treasury bills, notes and bonds are considered no risk. Triple A rated bonds are low risk. Equities (stocks) are considered to be higher risk. Some mutual fund portfolios combine both fixed-income investments and stocks.

The following table will give you an overview of how some people who invest for retirement balance risks depending upon age. Keep in mind that this chart considers investing in financial instruments only. Real estate and insurance are discussed in later chapters.

| Age | % in Risk categories | | |
	No risk	Low risk	Higher risk
40–49	0	60	40
50–59	10	60	30
60–69	40	40	20
70–79	60	30	10

As the chart suggests, as you grow older, you ought to consider taking less risk. People in their forties can consider taking more risks, even with retirement money, to build up their capital. Even if they lose on some of their investments, they have time to make it up. After age 50, you have less chance to make up any losses you may incur on stocks or on the higher risk types of mutual funds. As people move into their sixties they should take even less risk. How much depends on their risk tolerance, which should be measured at least once each year.

You will note that even at age 70+, some higher-risk investments are included. They offer you the best chance for capital appreciation, which is needed to offset inflation and growing expenses.

Will our current environment—relatively high interest rates and relatively low inflation—continue forever? Not likely. History says that over time equities out-perform fixed-income securities. As you have seen, even relatively low inflation erodes values. The real message is to stay flexible. Change your investment mix to suit the times as well as to fit your age and your feelings about risk.

CHANGING THE MIX

You should not make sudden changes in your investment mix. When you make quick shifts, you may sell high total return stocks that still have potential to grow. In addition, when you sell out a category of investment all at once, you may incur capital gains tax. Beware of advisers or planners who blithely tell you to sell out all, or a great majority of, your common stocks, and put the proceeds into safer, fixed-income investments such as Treasury bills, notes, or bonds, or tax-free municipals.

Suppose you have $100,000 of a common stock that you bought 20 years ago for $20,000. If you sell it, you will pay federal, state, and perhaps local capital gains tax on $80,000. In some jurisdictions, that could come to $32,000. Now you have just $68,000 to invest in Treasury bills or tax-free municipals. Your worth has dropped by $32,000, and what you have left must produce over 30 percent more than the current return on your $100,000 just to break even. That may be possible, but be sure to do the arithmetic before you make the change and remember that you are also giving up the chance for further growth of principal.

The best way to change the mix is to commit new money to the parts of the mix that you want to increase. Suppose, for example, when you reach your sixties, you have in your portfolio a municipal bond that matures. Rather than putting the money received from the bond back into municipals, which are low risk, invest in no-risk Treasury securities to achieve a new balance among your holdings.

In the case of common stocks, clean up your portfolio by selling securities in the same risk and capital gains category in which you have a loss. Losses that exactly offset gains eliminate capital gains taxes. Reinvest the proceeds of these sales in a different risk category to change your risk percentages. Gradual moves preserve your capital while achieving the new mix you want.

Immediate income

Usually, until you reach retirement age, you should forego taking dividends and interest in cash and should reinvest them. You can also accept low cash income in favor of returns that include growth. After you retire, you may have to go after the higher cash income that fixed-income securities usually offer.

Hedging your bets

Diversifying your investments among various types of investment vehicles is one of the best approaches to limiting your risks. It's also easy. You just spread your money around.

Mutual funds give you diversity and hedge your bets. The fund's manager takes over the complicated job of managing a large portfolio of stocks, bonds, or a mixture of both.

Dollar cost averaging is also a technique used to hedge bets primarily by long-term investors who, along with many professionals, believe it is impossible to "time" the stock market. You simply invest the same amount of money in a stock or mutual fund on a regular basis. The table shows you the results of dollar cost averaging versus buying a fixed number of shares on a regular basis. It assumes a total investment of $4,500 over a period of five quarters in a stock whose price fluctuates (wildly, in this example so as to stress the principle) between $3 and $15.

INVESTING A FIXED DOLLAR SUM VS. BUYING A FIXED NUMBER OF SHARES

	With dollar cost averaging			Without dollar cost averaging		
Purchased in (Quarter)	Cost per share	Number of shares purchased	Amount invested	Cost per share	Number of shares purchased	Amount invested
1Q	$ 6	150	$ 900	$ 6	100	$ 600
2Q	3	300	900	3	100	300
3Q	9	100	900	9	100	900
4Q	15	60	900	15	100	1,500
1Q	12	75	900	12	100	1,200
Totals		685	$4,500		500	$4,500

Table by Oppenheimer Fund Management Inc.

Using dollar cost averaging, a total of $4,500 at the rate of $900 each quarter acquires 685 shares at an average cost of $6.57 per share. The same sum of money invested to buy 100 shares at a time acquires only 500 shares at an average cost of $9 a share. Assume that the price of the stock becomes $10 a share. The value of the stock purchased using dollar cost averaging reaches $6,850 against $5,000 using the method of purchasing a fixed number of shares.

Dollar cost averaging may also lower your risk when the price trends go down. If you recast the figures in the table to show a downward trend, you will find that you lose less with dollar cost averaging than you would if you purchased a fixed number of shares each time you invested.

You can also lessen your risks by using "stop-loss" orders

on marketable securities kept in an account with a broker. You are not guaranteed that your sell order will be executed at exactly the amount you order. Sometimes the trader has so many sell orders that the price may slip a few points below your stop order before he or she can sell.

HOW TO INVEST

Basically, you have two choices: You can make your investment decisions yourself or you can hire people who specialize in planning and/or managing other people's money.

Mutual funds

The simplest way to get experts to manage your money is with a mutual fund. A mutual fund pools your money with that of many other investors. The fund manager then decides when, how much, and in what types of securities the fund will invest.

Many books have been written about mutual funds. If you plan to take that route, start checking them out. The main types of mutual funds are growth stock funds, balanced funds that mix stocks and bonds, income funds that are bonds alone, and tax-exempt bond funds that purchase only tax-exempt securities.

Because there are literally thousands of funds, you should take as much care in selecting a fund or funds for your retirement money as you would in selecting an individual stock. Well-known publications such as *Forbes*, *Business Week*, *Fortune,* and *Money* devote issues each year to rating the funds on their performance in all markets.

Also, professional services such as Wiesenberger Investment Companies Services evaluate funds. Their publications are usually available in the reference section of your library or in a broker's office.

To load or not to load. Another factor to consider when comparing mutual funds is load or no-load. About two-thirds of all funds charge a commission (or load), either upon purchase (front-end load) or on sale (back-end load). When you pay a commission of, say, 5 percent to invest $10,000 in a front-end load mutual fund, the fund puts only $9,500 of your money to work. With a no-load fund, you get the full $10,000 put to work right away.

Studies have shown, however, that over a five-year period, the return from load funds equals that of the no-loads because of higher management costs and fees that no-loads tend to charge.

It doesn't take much money to start buying mutual funds. Some will let you buy for as little as a $500 initial investment. Usually you can make additional investments of as little as $25. By law the fund or broker is required to give you a prospectus before you buy. The prospectus must describe the fund's investment philosophies, policies, and costs. You will find a phone number to call to get answers to your questions. Do not hesitate to call. The only dumb question is the one you didn't ask.

Once you are in a fund, keep careful records of how much you paid for it and, if you are reinvesting dividends, how much the dividends were and what they bought.

Doing it yourself

You must be willing to learn about personal investing if you decide to manage your funds yourself. You can find many books on the subject. High schools and community colleges run adult education classes on investing and there are numerous seminars and college and correspondence courses available.

Once you know the fundamentals, you should devote at least a couple of hours a week to keeping up to date on the markets and your particular securities. That's easy to do with torrents of information pouring out of daily newspapers, radio, TV, and business and financial publications.

Here are some "don'ts" to guide you when you are managing your own personal investments:

☐ Don't buy anything you do not understand no matter who tells you about it. It may not fit your goals; it may be too volatile for your personal risk tolerance. Never be hurried by statements like "You've got to get in this today or you won't have another

TAXABLE VERSUS TAX-FREE YIELDS

When making a choice between investing in a tax-exempt security or a taxable one, do not make the mistake of avoiding taxes just to avoid them. What you are interested in is the after-tax return. Suppose you are in a 28 percent federal and 8 percent state tax bracket. Here's how you would analyze a tax-exempt yield of $7^1/2$ percent from a municipal bond issued in your state:

1. Because state taxes are deductible from federal taxes, calculate your effective state tax. Simply multiply 8 percent by 72 percent (100% minus your federal tax rate of 28 percent).

That calculation is .08 x .72 = .057

2. Add your effective state tax to your federal tax:

28% + 5.7% = 33.7%.

3. Use this formula:

$$\frac{7^1/2\%}{66.3\%(100\%-33.7\%)} = 11.3\%$$

If you can get a taxable yield of more than 11.3 percent, you are better off than you are with the $7^1/2$ percent tax-free yield. Naturally, you must also always consider the safety factor when making such decisions.

chance." There is always time to make a good investment.

☐ Don't let taxes drive you. You hear a great deal about tax-free investments, mostly municipal bonds that are not subject to federal, state, and local taxes. They sound great and certainly appeal to most people's dislike of paying taxes. The problem is, in their hurry to escape taxes, buyers of tax exempts may ignore fundamental weaknesses in the securities themselves. In the last few years, more than $1 billion in municipal bonds have defaulted. Moreover, some people do not calculate equivalent tax yield and accept a lower after-tax return by investing in tax frees than they would get if they invested in taxable securities.

- [ ] Don't judge a security solely on past performance. It might have had a fantastic increase in one year out of the last ten, making it appear to have done well. You're not investing in the past. What you want to assess is the chance for future performance.
- [ ] Don't reach for tiny fractions of interest or dividend return.
- [ ] Don't get hung up on when to commit your funds. As the dollar cost averaging example shows, if you pick the right investment vehicle, you can start any time just so long as you commit the same dollar amount regularly.
- [ ] Don't invest retirement money in securities on which you cannot quickly obtain a price quote and turn that quote into an immediate sale. You should not tie up retirement money, other than your home, in assets that you can't quickly turn into cash for emergencies.

SAFE INVESTMENTS

Unless Uncle Sam himself goes belly up, there is no safer investment than United States Treasury securities. The Treasury issues three types of debt obligations: bills, notes, and bonds. The main distinction among them is how long they will be outstanding until maturity. Bills mature in 13, 26, and 52 weeks. You must buy at least a $10,000 bill, but you can go for more in multiples of $5,000. These are sold at a discount, so that a 52-week $10,000 bill with an 8% interest rate would cost you $9,200. When the bill matures, you get the full $10,000. Because you are getting $800 on an investment of $9,200, your actual yield is 8.7%, not 8%.

Treasury notes are sold with maturities of two, three, four, five, and seven years. You can lend Uncle Sam (for that's exactly what you are doing when you buy treasuries) as little as $1,000, though those that mature in less than four years usually require you to put up $5,000.

Treasury bonds have maturities of 10 to 30 years. They, too, can be bought in as little as $1,000 denominations. Bills, notes and bonds are highly liquid—not through the Treasury, though. Brokers and dealers ensure an active market in them. You will pay a commission if you sell before maturity. Both Treasury notes and bonds make regular semi-annual interest payments.

The latest wrinkle in treasuries is known as Treasury Direct. When you establish such an account, the interest (and, later, principal, if you do not roll it over) on your Treasury securities will be sent electronically to a bank account that starts earning interest immediately. You pay no commissions when using a Treasury Direct Account. If there is a drawback to the system, it comes up when you wish to sell, trade, or pledge the Treasury security before maturity. You have to fill out a special form to transfer it to another system. Such a transfer can take two weeks.

To get comprehensive information about buying and other details, call the Federal Reserve Bank nearest you or the Treasury Bureau of Public Debt (Washington, DC 20239-1000; (202) 287-4113). Or, send for an excellent 76-page booklet called "Buying Treasury Securities at Federal Reserve Banks" from the Federal Reserve Bank of Richmond (P.O. Box 27471, Richmond, VA 23261). Enclose payment of $4.50. It 's worth it.

ALMOST SAFE INVESTMENTS

Triple A (AAA) rated corporate and municipal bonds are suitable for investment of retirement funds. Municipal bonds are exempt from federal taxes and usually from state and local taxes, providing you are a resident of the state in which the municipality is located.

Municipals and corporate bonds, like all fixed-income securities, may decline in value when interest rates rise. Should you have to sell them before maturity, you could incur a loss. Even though you will get back the dollar denomination of a bond at maturity, even mild inflation can erode its buying power.

STOCKS

Many stocks deserve to be included in retirement funds because of their long records of dividend payments, growth, and total return.

Some investment in stocks or stock mutual funds is needed for growth. How much depends upon your risk tolerance.

Because of fluctuations in the prices of common stocks, you should watch them carefully. Keep up to date through your weekly investment reading on how the company or mutual fund you have invested in is faring. Be prepared to act promptly should you learn of any trouble.

As an investor, you must recognize that money is made or lost as often for psychological reasons as through the success or failure of companies. Knowledge of securities and of the markets must be supplemented by caution. Cultivate purely objective approaches to the matter of buying and selling securities.

Assuming that sufficient attention is given to the analysis of securities, as an investor you should trust the facts. Distrust mere opinions, beliefs, or guesses. Get to know yourself well enough to discern when your judgments on investing are based on bravery and when they are pushed by bravado.

CHAPTER VI

Ensuring retirement income through insurance

There is no such thing as a perfect retirement investment. If there were, it would have such characteristics as safety, liquidity, high income, good growth potential, and tax advantages. You would probably also prefer something that does not take a lot of time and energy to manage. Is there anything like that out there? Today, certain kinds of insurance company products claim all those features.

A lot of people still think of life insurance as something they will never be around to enjoy. That's true for term life insurance, which provides only a death benefit. For dozens of other life insurance products, though, nothing could be further from the truth.

The fact is that insurance products, after dawdling along in the rear of the investment parade for 30 years, have made a real comeback during the past decade. Today many types of policies provide very competitive rates of return. They combine that benefit with safety, tax advantages, ease of management, and flexibility.

Two broad categories of insurance products should be considered for retirement planning. They are the newer types of life insurance policies described in the chart on page 53; and annuities, which provide monthly payments for the life of the individuals who are covered by them. They are more fully described later in the chapter.

BASICS ABOUT LIFE INSURANCE

In contrast to term insurance, permanent insurance offers protection for your whole life with no increase in premiums. The insurance company accomplishes this by charging higher premiums than those for term insurance in the early years and building up a reserve to help pay premiums in later years, when premiums on term policies start to rise dramatically.

All permanent life policies offer protection against death (the death benefit) coupled with a savings or investment account (cash values). In other words, you can get something back whether you live or die. What's more, the cash value within the policy grows on a tax-deferred basis, so that income taxes on the gain do not have to be paid unless and until the policy is cashed in.

Whole life

Whole life, or ordinary life, or straight life—all different names for the same product—is the best known type of permanent insurance. Whole life offers a guaranteed premium and death benefit. If you die, the policy pays the face amount of insurance to your beneficiary. It also provides a guaranteed minimum cash value, which is like a savings account within the policy. In addition, many policies pay dividends that, if reinvested, can increase your cash value substantially. Dividends are technically a partial return of premium, so they are not taxable.

You can borrow or withdraw against or the cash value of your policy if necessary, although there are limits to how much you can withdraw. If you purchased the policy before June 21, 1988, you can borrow or withdraw from it tax-free. If you bought it after that date, you will have to ask the company what tests your policy must meet to make loans or withdrawals tax-free. You can also cancel the policy and get back the cash value, a useful option for people who want to supplement retirement income. Such settlement options include converting the cash value into an annuity.

HOW PERMANENT POLICIES DIFFER

	Policy provides	Values to policyholder	Death benefits
Traditional whole life	Fixed premium payments but can borrow on cash values to pay Guaranteed cash values	Policyholder can borrow against cash value/ dividends or withdraw dividends Dividends can be paid in cash, can reduce premiums, or can buy more paid-up insurance	Guaranteed death benefit which can increase from dividends purchasing paid-up insurance
Universal life	Policyholder can adjust premiums Cash values vary with interest rate performance	Insurance company invests cash value at a current interest rate, but policy provides for a minimum rate of return Policyholder can borrow against or make partial withdrawals	Guaranteed minimum death benefit, but can otherwise be varied by policyholder
Variable life	Fixed premium payment but can borrow on cash values to pay Cash values vary with fund performance with risk to policyholder	Policyholder chooses from various funds to invest cash values Policyholder can borrow against cash values Generally no interest rate guarantees	Variable, but not lower than original face amount of policy
Variable universal life	Policyholder can vary premium amounts paid Cash values vary with fund performance	Policyholder chooses investment fund to invest cash values Policyholder can borrow against cash values or make withdrawals Interest rate varies with fund performance	Guaranteed minimum death benefit, not lower than the original face amount of the policy Policyholder can vary death benefit, which may also vary with fund performance

INTEREST-SENSITIVE POLICIES

A few years ago, thanks to competition and a changing investment environment, interest-sensitive permanent life insurance products were introduced. The main distinguishing feature of interest-sensitive contracts is that they separate the insurance portion (the protection part) from the investment portion (the savings part). With interest-sensitive products you are assuming more risk than with a traditional whole life policy. In return, you may enjoy greater investment returns.

Universal life

With this interest-sensitive policy, you can have flexible premium payments and there is a minimum guaranteed death benefit and interest rate. When a premium is paid, some expense charges may be deducted and the balance is put into your investment account.

Universal life allows you to change the mix of the policy to meet your needs. In the early years, you may emphasize a high death benefit to protect your family. Later you may choose a lower death benefit and, at the same time, a buildup of earnings for greater retirement income.

With universal life you can not only vary the amount of the premiums paid but also omit paying them entirely. If you omit payments, the insurer dips into the cash fund's investment for the money to continue the death benefit. If there is not enough there, the death benefit decreases.

Variable life

A variable life policy allows you to pick the type of investment you want. For the investment account, you typically can choose among money market, stock, bond, and real estate funds. You can also periodically change the balance of investments in your account. As with all policies, there is a guaranteed death benefit, but there is no minimum guaranteed cash value.

Variable universal life

This combines features of both variable and universal products.

A variable universal life contract offers flexible premiums (as in a universal policy) as well as the ability to direct how your investment is invested (as with variable).

Single premium life

This can be either a single premium whole life policy or a variable life policy. You pay one premium and immediately get a paid-up contract. You never have to make another premium payment for the insurance coverage. The advantages are that the investment grows on a tax-deferred basis and, like traditional insurance products, the death benefit is tax-free. The disadvantage is that new tax regulations (on policies issued after June 21, 1987) penalize many types of withdrawals from single premium policies, so you do not have ready access to your investment until age $59^1/2$.

ANNUITIES

An annuity is a contract in which you pay a sum of money to an insurance company, which then guarantees you a monthly income, either for a specified number of years or for your lifetime. Annuities sold by life insurance companies require no physical exam. You can purchase annuities at almost any age, though you should be cautious about buying them after you have passed, say, age 75. They are designed for individuals who are more concerned about outliving their financial reserves than they are about providing death benefits to their estates or survivors.

Most people want part of their retirement income coming in like clockwork each month. Annuities do that. More importantly, they can provide you with the security of having an income you will never outlive. You can also choose an annuity that will continue, after your death, to make lifetime payments to your spouse

You can buy an annuity through annual premium payments. Or, if you should receive a substantial sum of money all at once—an inheritance, or a fairly large annual bonus—you can

Real life, real answers.

Fifty-year-old Tom Lydecker is faced with a pleasant dilemma. The new bonus system set up by the aerospace company he works for in Ogden, Utah, promises to boost his income by at least $5,000 per year after taxes for the next decade.

Since Tom and his wife Marilyn live fairly comfortably on his salary, they decide to earmark that bonus income for their retirement. But where should they put it?

They explore and compare two programs. The first is a series of CDs, a new one with each year's bonus check. This is nice safe investment with a guaranteed return. At 8 percent the CDs will earn $22,880 compounded interest by end of year 10. But if they do that, Tom will end up paying income tax each year on the interest. At his current state and federal tax rate, that amounts to $6,754. That is $6,754 that could have gone into other investments rather than into Uncle Sam's pocket.

The second option is a straight annuity investment, $5,000 every year in a separate single premium deferred annuity (SPDA), at 8 percent. In 10 years the Lydeckers would have put away $50,000 and paid no income tax on the $22,880 of earnings. The Lydeckers' nest egg would be worth $72,880 by the time Tom is 60, an advantage over the CDs of $6,754, as the chart below shows.

	Compounded interest at year 10	Federal and state tax at 30%	Value at year 10	Increased value advantage
CDs	$22,880	$6,754	$66,126	none
Single premium deferred annuity	22,880	none	72,880	$6,754

Tom must keep in mind, though, that if he purchases the SPDAs or any contract that defers income tax, he cannot withdraw cash until he is age 59$^{1}/_{2}$ without incurring a 10 percent penalty tax in addition to regular income tax. That is not the case with CDs.

Tom and Marilyn Lydecker opted for the annuity.

buy a single premium annuity with one lump-sum payment. Annuities are ideal for deferring taxes on the earnings generated after they are invested.

Deferring taxes

You can contribute up to $2,000 each year to an IRA. What if your bonus comes to $7,500? Or you receive an inheritance of $25,000? When you buy an annuity from a life insurance company, you are not restricted to a maximum contribution. Generally, you need only fork over a minimum of $2,500.

Bear in mind that you will not pay income taxes on the annuity's earnings until you start to draw out cash. Of course, there is no tax on the money you contributed to the annuity because the company is simply returning your capital. When you do annuitize, that is, start taking monthly payments, you will pay tax only on part of the payments received over your lifetime, since part of each payment will be a return of your costs.

Choosing the right annuity

You can buy several types of annuities: deferred, immediate, fixed, or variable—with a plethora of permutations.

A deferred annuity starts paying you at a specified future age, though you can change your mind and have smaller payments begun earlier if you wish. You can buy it with one lump sum (single premium) or in installments.

An immediate annuity starts paying you immediately and requires you to pay its premium up front.

A fixed annuity guarantees you a fixed monthly payment for your life or for a set number of years (or whichever is longer—known as X years certain). The amount of the payment depends on your age and when payments start.

In a *variable annuity*, the insurance company invests in a group of securities, such as corporate bonds, treasuries, and stocks. How much you get paid each month for life depends on how well the portfolio performs. Some variable annuities do not guarantee return of the entire principal (you can buy variable annuities that do); variable annuities do not guarantee the interest rate, or income. Their values are tied to the perform-ance of the underlying investments. Their purpose is to provide higher income than annuities with specific guarantees. The higher the risk, the higher the potential rewards.

If you are a public school teacher or work for certain other nonprofit institutions, you can buy a tax-deferred annuity with pretax income. This makes it is a particularly attractive option for retirement. Ask your employer if you are eligible.

Saving money

You might pay sales commissions to buy annuities, in which case you have less money growing from the start. Some types of annuities also have fees for investment management and other costs that can drain as much as 2.5 points a year from the income return. Shop around to get the best rates and the lowest fees. Payouts of insurance companies vary as widely as 20 percent, so shop carefully.

If you have a sudden need for cash or a change of mind about keeping an annuity during the early years, you will usually incur a bailout fee. Find out exactly how long you have to wait before you can get your money without paying a fee. Also re-member that cashing in an annuity before age $59\frac{1}{2}$ triggers a 10 percent penalty tax by Uncle Sam. That's why it is so impor-tant to think of annuities as long-term investments.

Some firms offer very high initial interest rates as bait to pull you in. Find out how long the company guarantees the "come-and-get-me" rate. It could be three months or three years. Uncover the guaranteed interest rate, the record of excess interest credited, and decide if you can live with that return.

When you buy variable annuities, keep in mind that the mutual fund return can go down as well as up. That's true even with fixed-income funds that invest in bonds. Their value goes down when interest rates go up and vice versa.

You don't get much of a death benefit for the cost when you buy single premium annuities. But small is better than none, and it is the safety factors, lifetime payments, and tax advantages for which people really buy annuities.

Find out what happens should you contribute a large sum to an annuity and die only a couple of years after you start drawing out cash. You will have structured your payments for your life or for a fixed number of years. So, in several years you would be paid back only a small fraction of the amount you have invested. Some states mandate how much must be paid to your heirs or estate. Normally, if you die before your invested interest in the contract is fully paid out, the remaining portion of your investment will be paid to your beneficiary at least as rapidly as the annuity called for. It is possible to contract for a lump-sum payout to your estate or heirs, though that may not be the best deal from a tax point of view.

Should you buy an annuity that later compares unfavorably to new ones, you can switch to a better annuity without being subject to a 10 percent excise tax. You must, however, follow the rules of the Internal Revenue Service to escape penalty.

Above all, shop, shop, shop. You wouldn't buy a car without shopping around. So, do not buy annuities without kicking some life insurance company tires first.

TIPS FOR PROFIT AND SAFETY

For annuities, find a company that will:

1. Let you get at your money without a surrender fee.
2. Give you a very competitive interest rate.
3. Let you buy with no front-end costs.
4. Guarantee 100 percent return of the amount you have invested.

In addition, the company should be rated A+ or A with A. M. Best Company. A. M. Best publishes ratings of more than 1,000 insurance companies in its publication *Best's Insurance Reports*. Many libraries carry it in their reference sections. Search until you find it. You want to be sure that the insurance company survives you.

CHAPTER VII

Real estate: powerful retirement income provider

R eal estate offers retirement planners a strong hedge against inflation, a sound way to diversify their nest eggs, and a potential post-retirement income producer. You can invest in real estate by becoming a landlord if you have the time and the temperament for it. Or you can take a hands-off investment approach by putting a portion of your portfolio into real estate investment vehicles.

The most common way to get some kind of retirement income from real estate is through investment in your own home. This chapter will concentrate on that aspect of retirement planning. But first, a brief look at real estate investing outside your own home.

BECOMING A LANDLORD

Many individuals planning for retirement see a rentable home or a small commercial or apartment building as a safe investment to make their money grow. They look to become landlords. Whether you buy an apartment building with four rentals or a house you rent to one person, the principles are the same. You get a regular source of income from the rentals (after all costs) that tends to rise with inflation. You get a second inflation hedge from the tendency of real estate to appreciate in value.

The latter is the key. Real estate is basically a long-term financial commitment. It offers one of the few options in which inflation is on your side. High rents and increasing home values are sparked by inflation; they put more money in your pocket— eventually.

But being a landlord is no picnic. You have to pick the right house at the right price, get the right tenants, and perhaps suffer slow rental periods. You have to know how to take advantage of depreciation and tax breaks that a real estate investment offers, and be prepared to spend at least a day a month with TAT—toilets and tenants—problems, repairs, collecting rent, etc. You also have to deal with local laws, giving notice, upkeep, and deposits.

INVESTING IN REITs

The hands-off approach could mean investing in a real estate investment trust. Your money is pooled with that of other investors, and under the management of a real estate professional, it is invested in income-producing properties—apartment buildings, office buildings, warehouses, etc. REITs have advantages and disadvantages. They boast annual cash payouts with substantial dividends, like utility stocks. Also, like utilities, they are interest-rate sensitive, tending to move down when rates rise and vice versa.

Individuals seeking income are enticed by the requirement that REITs distribute 95 percent of their earnings to investors each year. But there are also management fees, expenses, etc., that come out of the pot first. The drop in individual tax rates makes cash payments more appealing. But Uncle Sam is still going to get his.

Different REITs have different portfolios. Before you send a check to one, check the following:

☐ Average yield for publicly traded REITs.
☐ Portfolios with particular mixes that you see doing well in the future (for example, industrial warehouses in smokestack cities).
☐ Whether the REIT has high debt or leverage (it should have solid income and good cash flow).

- How successful previous offerings by the REIT have been.
- How much of your investment buys property, how much goes to fees.
- All fees involved: up-front, continuing, and liquidation.
- Whether you can afford a REIT for diversification to serve as a long-term hedge against inflation.

For more information on REITs, see your broker, or go to your public library and look them up in the *Value Line Investment Service* or *Standard & Poor's Stock Reports*.

USING YOUR HOME TO PROVIDE RETIREMENT INCOME

If you are one of the lucky ones who bought a house 30 years ago and has watched it appreciate in value to a multiple of five, seven, or even ten times what you paid for it, you are living in what is your number one asset and the best single investment you ever made. By now, whatever mortgage payments you have left are miniscule in comparison to what the house is worth.

You are faced with one of the key decisions of retirement: Stay or go?

Some people know they want to move to a smaller house in a better climate. Others may want to stay in the same area but move into a hassle-free condominium. Still others want nothing more than to stay in the same house they have lived in for years. Whatever your choice, there are ways for you to use the equity in your home to provide needed retirement income.

Selling and buying a less expensive home

If you are planning to sell and move, you will be able to take advantage of the one-time, over-55, $125,000 tax exemption.

As long as one owner of the house is over 55, you get a capital gains exclusion of $125,000 on the profit you make from selling your house (the one-time requirement covers both sellers regardless of age). It's a good deal, but there's a good deal more you should know.

Real life, real answers.

George and Rosalie Smythe bought their home 50 miles outside New York City in 1959. Their one-acre, eight-room ranch cost $35,000 and over the years they enclosed the porch, put a bar and playroom in the basement, had patios built in both the front and back, and put on a new roof.

By the 1970's, the Smythes had paid off the college loans for their three children and begun to think about retirement. George would retire from his insurance agency at 65 and Rosalie would give up her part-time library position. Their ultimate dream: Buy a small two-bedroom home on Cape Cod. After extensive shopping, they found a non-beachfront cottage that needed a lot of work, which was fine for the handy George.

He put his suburban home on the market in 1989 for $275,000 and settled for $255,000. His records showed that the capital improvements they had made cost $60,000. Added to the $35,000 purchase price, that made their basis $95,000. The difference—$160,000—was not taxable because the Smythes took the $125,000 one-time exclusion and paid more than $35,000 for a new house.

In fact, the Smythes paid $115,000 for their dream house and sank in another $20,000 to tailor it to their tastes. They used the remaining $120,000 ($255,000 minus $135,000) to buy an annuity that paid enough every month to cover taxes, utilities, and maintenance of their new home.

You must have used the house as your primary residence for three of the last five years. You get to use this exemption only once, so you want to make sure you can use as much of the $125,000 exclusion as possible. In figuring your gain, subtract from the selling price your original cost of the house, closing costs, and capital improvements.

Keep in mind the real estate rollover rule. If you sell your house and use the money to buy another that costs the same (or more), that effectively postpones taxes. Thus, you do not have to use your exclusion because there is no gain.

Selling a primary residence, buying a smaller and less expensive home, and investing the money gained for a source of income is one of the most common scenarios for couples planning retirement.

Home equity conversions

There are other ways to convert the equity you have built into your home into cash. All involve using your home as collateral to borrow money, and paying interest on it.

No matter what home equity conversion route you take, you want it explained in terms you understand and in a logical manner so you can compare one plan with another. Key areas to investigate:

- ☐ Initial cash payment to you.
- ☐ Monthly payments: amount, term, duration.
- ☐ Expected schedule of payments, if interest or payment level is adjusted.
- ☐ In the case of variable interest rates, the effect of a specific rate change (for example from 12 percent to 14 percent) on payments and loan balance.
- ☐ Tax status of payments.
- ☐ Equity position of the homeowner at the end of term or after a specified period of time, including the loan balance attributable to interest and principal.
- ☐ The amount and terms of any annuity.
- ☐ Any prepayment penalties or penalties for revoking the agreement.
- ☐ The disposal of the property at the end of term or reappraisal of property value.

Pros and cons of home equity loans

Basically, a home equity loan is a second mortgage against your house. The maximum you can borrow is usually 70 to 80 percent of the difference between the appraisal value of your house and your mortgage balance.

You can take your money out in a lump sum or in stages, but you start repaying as soon as you start using it. You also pay a pretty penny to have that money at your beck and call. Among the fees: origination (points as high as 2 percent), appraisal and credit, title search and insurance, surveys, mortgage taxes, recordings, revolving credit title endorsement, attorneys' fees, plus an interest rate pegged to the prime.

If you do opt for such a loan, shop around for your best buy and try to get that interest rate fixed, not variable. And make sure you will not suffer penalties if you eventually prepay.

If you are finally seeing the light at the end of your mortgage payment tunnel, why would you pile a new loan obligation on your income? For one thing, you can use the money for any purpose: home improvement to increase the value of the home you will eventually sell; purchase of a second home that you will live in once you retire; unexpected medical expenses; a one-time investment opportunity that requires up-front cash, etc.

For another, you can find interest rates that are lower than other types of consumer credit, like personal loans, and significantly lower than credit card rates, if you decide to pay off a major purchase made on one of them. The big payoff is that the interest is still tax-deductible on a home equity loan. However, points are no longer immediately deductible, but must be spread out over the life of the loan.

Strategies

Watch out for major differences between home equity *loans* and home equity *lines of credit.* The latter often use variable interest rates. They are too easy to use and too hard to repay. They are not suitable for financial planning for a secure retirement.

In addition, do not overlook the strategy known as prepayment. It can, for example, turn a long mortgage into a shorter one, and high total interest expenses into a lower amount. You need to work out a prepayment schedule that satisfies both you and your lender, but basically the strategy works as follows:

Instead of paying the standard monthly amount on your mortgage or other long-term debt, you add a sweetener. Maybe $25, the cost of one inexpensive dinner for two once a month. On a regular basis, that prepayment will eat away at what you owe at a faster rate, thanks to reduction of accumulated interest and compounding.

Reverse mortgages

Another home equity conversion vehicle is a reverse mortgage (RM), the opposite of a conventional mortgage. You receive monthly payments based on the amount of home equity borrowed against, interest rate, and length of loan. You can usually repay it at any time. Or it may be liquidated by your death or sale of the house.

Reverse mortgages are not everyone's cup of tea. They appeal to people who are house rich, but money poor. They offer access to cash. Loan advances are not taxable. The income does not affect Social Security or Medicare. And you take active advantage of an asset—your house—that might otherwise lie dormant.

On the other hand, you use up some or all of the equity you have worked so hard to build into your home. The eventual cost may be greater than that of other special purpose loans. Interest is compounded, creating a situation in which total accumulated interest could even exceed principal drawn down. You must pay all those up-front fees, just as you did when you closed on your house. The interest on the RM is not deductible on your income taxes until you pay it all off. And most important to many people, you do not retain the right to leave your house to your heirs. But an RM is a way to enable you to stay in a house you might otherwise be forced to sell.

Here's what a typical RM might look like from the bottom line. You ask for $250,000 for 10 years at 10.5 percent interest with an initial lump-sum payment of $20,000. You get a little over $900 per month for 10 years, when you would owe $128,960 in principal and $121,040 in interest.

The length of the loan naturally affects the amount of cash you borrow. The longer the term, the less you get. The same is true of the interest rate you pay. The higher it is, the lower the monthly payments you receive. For a fixed term RM, you need to consider how long you need the money coming in, how much you need each pay period, how you will repay when the loan comes due, and how much equity you want to retain (perhaps in anticipation of paying the loan off).

The majority of reverse mortgages have a series of common characteristics.

1. All are rising debt loans. That means the total you owe increases over time.
2. Money paid to you depends on the value of your home, the amount of equity you borrow against, the interest rate, and the length of the loan.
3. You can request an initial lump sum—useful for postponed repairs, an added bathroom, etc.
4. The loan is due when you die, permanently move, or sell (or on a set date in case of term).
5. Your legal obligations are limited to the value of your house. If you owe more, your personal assets cannot be attached.
6. You keep the title to your house, but lose it if you do not repay at the end of the term.
7. There is no prepayment penalty.

Sale/leaseback

In a sale/leaseback or life tenancy arrangement, you sell your home to an investor but retain the right to live in it as a renter. The investor normally takes on the obligation for insurance, taxes, and repairs. He or she also pays the former owner a lump sum or monthly stipend based on the cost of the house, less an agreed upon rental fee. Basically, this is a match of an owner in need of cash and an investor looking for tax breaks and real estate investments.

Sometimes the investor sets up a deferred payment annuity to cover monthly income to you after the original price of the house (in principal and interest) has been paid. Or you may set up your own annuity. You stay in your house, receive monthly payments, and no longer worry about taxes, major maintenance, repairs, etc.

You can use your one-time, over-55, $125,000 house-selling exemption to lower tax liability on your capital gains. You will also have a much better fix on your monthly finances, both inflow and outgo, with a sale/leaseback arrangement. The big drawbacks are that you lose the house as part of your estate and lose out on any further appreciation on it over the years.

Home equity conversions will give you an infusion of income, but they eventually drain away the investment in your house. Weigh the impact on your personal situation. No matter what type of home equity conversion you decide to undertake, get help from the professionals. Here are three places to start: AARP, Home Equity Information Center (1909 K Street, N.W., Washington, DC 20049); National Center for Home Equity Conversion (110 E. Main Street, Room 1010, Madison, WI 53703); Federal Housing Authority (FHA) at (800) 245-2691 for lenders in your area involved in reverse mortgage programs.

CHAPTER VIII

Health care after retirement: staying financially healthy

The challenge today is preparing for tomorrow's health needs, when you do not know what they will be. You have seen all the headlines about skyrocketing health costs. How do they fit into that secure retirement financial plan you are developing?

To get your health cost bearings in sight, focus on four major areas—Medicare/Medicaid; the controversial Catastrophic Health Care coverage; Medigap; and long-term care (LTC) insurance policies. As you read, keep in mind that this a rapidly changing area. Laws that will affect government-funded health care are constantly being considered. Private nursing home insurance is a new and evolving industry as well.

YOUR CURRENT HEALTH INSURANCE

Start with the health insurance benefits you have enjoyed at your place of work. There are laws that govern employer-provided health insurance once you have obtained it. The main one that affects continuation and conversion rights once you leave your company is the Consolidated Omnibus Budget Reconciliation Act (COBRA). State laws may also apply, so ask your company's benefits consultant about them.

In general, COBRA requires organizations with group health insurance policies to continue coverage of former employees under certain conditions when they leave the company's employment or retire. The policies must offer the right to convert to individual policies once that continuation period (usually 18 to 36 months) expires. If your company offers any sort of continued benefits, they are likely to be cheaper and more comprehensive than anything you can acquire on your own.

The insurer can charge you no more than 102 percent of the group rate (100 percent for the coverage and 2 percent for administrative fees). You must, of course, make timely payments to keep your insurance in force. Some union contracts and executive benefit packages call for continuation of the company's practice of picking up all or part of health insurance for retirees.

If your old company's medical coverage is modified for the better, you get to take advantage of that too. You must be notified of your rights to continue coverage and be given 60 days to make up your mind.

One catch under COBRA: Continuation of basic coverage ends when you become entitled to Medicare benefits at 65. But you may still be eligible for some extended coverage.

MEDICARE

Medicare is a national health insurance program primarily for persons 65 and older. Enacted in 1965, it represents the major effort by our government to provide older citizens with some form of medical care. Almost every one of us becomes eligible for Medicare on our sixty-fifth birthday.* The important thing to remember about Medicare is that it is designed to pay for medical-related care only. It does not take care of all long-term care needs and is not really the "safety net" we hear so much about in the media.

Coverage is divided into two parts. Part A, also known as the "basic plan" or "hospital insurance," is largely financed by the Social Security tax on salaries. This hospital insurance helps

---

* A few exceptions—some state and local government workers, some railroad workers, and some people who have never worked are not covered by a spouse's benefits.

pay for medically necessary stays in participating hospitals, skilled nursing facilities, and hospices and for some home health care.

Part B coverage, known as "medical coverage," helps pay for medically necessary outpatient (that is, out-of-hospital) care by doctors and other medical specialists, such as physical and speech therapists. It also helps pay for some home health care and services.

Following is a summary of Medicare benefits. Because Congress was debating major changes in the 1988 Medicare Catastrophic Coverage Act as this book was going to press, you should consult *The Medicare Handbook*, an excellent free government publication, for the most up-to-date description of benefits and costs. The Medicare toll-free number is (800) 888-1998.

Part A—hospital insurance

Inpatient hospital services. In order to qualify for hospital coverage, you must meet *all* of the following conditions:

- ☐ The hospitalization must be prescribed by a doctor.
- ☐ The care you need can be provided only by a hospital.
- ☐ The hospital must *participate* in Medicare. This means that the hospital has agreed to accept Medicare's payment as the full payment for everything except your calendar-year deductible.
- ☐ The hospital's utilization review committee or peer review committee must not disapprove your stay. These committees are made up of doctors who practice at the hospital and who have the responsibility of reviewing admissions to make sure that everyone admitted really needs hospital care.

If you meet all four of these conditions, Medicare will pay for approved medically necessary inpatient hospital care after you pay a yearly deductible. These terms are defined as follows: A deductible is the dollar amount that you must pay. It is indexed for inflation each year. In 1990, it is approximately $580. *Medically necessary* is a term that means appropriate, reasonable, and necessary care as determined by your doctor, and not disapproved by peer review. *Warning*: Medicare pays for only limited inpatient psychiatric care.

Major inpatient hospital services:

☐ Semiprivate room.

☐ All meals, including special dietary needs.

☐ Regular nursing.

☐ Special units, such as operating and recovery rooms, anesthesia, and intensive care.

☐ Hospital-furnished drugs.

☐ Most blood transfusions.

☐ Hospital-billed X-ray and other radiology services.

☐ Medical supplies, such as casts.

☐ Use of appliances, such as wheelchairs.

☐ Rehabilitation therapy.

Services specifically excluded:

☐ Personal conveniences, such as televisions and telephones.

☐ Private-duty nurses.

Medically necessary inpatient skilled nursing home care. In order to qualify for Medicare coverage, not only must care take place in a skilled nursing home and be medically necessary, the nursing home must provide skilled care (as defined by Medicare) and be Medicare-approved. Remember, most nursing homes *do not* provide skilled care, and most skilled-care nursing homes *are not* Medicare-approved. In addition, a doctor must certify your need for restorative care and must certify that you are receiving such care on a daily basis. Finally, your stay must not be disapproved by an independent review organization.

The major allowable services include:

☐ A semiprivate room.

☐ All meals, including special dietary meals.

☐ Regular nursing.

☐ Nursing home-furnished drugs.

☐ Most blood transfusions.

☐ Medical supplies.

☐ Use of appliances.

Specifically not included:

☐ Personal conveniences.

☐ Private-duty nurses.

☐ Private-room charges.

Home Health Care. Home health-care coverage is contingent upon the following conditions:

☐ The care must be prescribed by a physician who must set up a home health plan for you.

☐ Your care must require intermittent skilled nursing care or physical or speech therapy.

☐ You must be confined to your home.

☐ The care must be provided by a Medicare-participating home health agency.

If these conditions are met, Medicare will pay for the full cost of:

☐ Part-time or intermittent skilled nursing care, speech, and physical therapy.

☐ Occupational therapy.

☐ A part-time or intermittent home health aide.

☐ Medical supplies.

☐ Eighty percent of the cost of certain medical equipment.

Medicare specifically will not cover:

☐ Full-time nursing at home.

☐ Drugs.

☐ Meals-on-Wheels.

☐ Homemaker services.

☐ Blood.

Part B—medical insurance

Reasonable Charges. Before you can understand Medicare coverage, it is necessary to define one important term used in Medicare legislation. *Reasonable charges* refers to the dollar amount for a particular medical service (such as a gall bladder operation) that Medicare will approve. Medicare arrives at this amount by using the lower of the following amounts:

The prevailing charge: that is, the customary charge for that particular service in that locality, or the doctor's or supplier's *actual charge*.

Deductible and Co-insurance. The *deductible* is the dollar amount (currently $75) that you must pay before Medicare will start paying. The *co-insurance* is the percent of your approved bill that Medicare will pay. That is now 80 percent. These are independent of the Part A deductible.

Medical Insurance Coverage. Doctors' bills, including the following, are covered:

☐ Medical and surgical services, including anesthesia and related diagnostic tests and procedures, inpatient and outpatient radiological and pathological services.

☐ Services provided at your doctor's office and included in his or her bill, such as:

  ☐ Services of the office nurse.
  ☐ Drugs you cannot administer yourself.
  ☐ Transfusions.
  ☐ Medical supplies.
  ☐ Therapy (physical, occupational, and speech).

Outpatient hospital services are covered at participating hospitals. These include:

☐ Emergency room and outpatient clinics.
☐ Lab tests, radiological services, and medical supplies.
☐ Drugs you cannot administer yourself.
☐ Outpatient blood transfusions.

  Major services specifically excluded:

☐ Routine physical exams and related tests.
☐ Exams for glasses or hearing aids.
☐ Most immunizations.
☐ Most cosmetic surgery.
☐ Routine foot care.

Nursing care and home health aid are covered for seven days per week with one or more visits per day for a maximum of 38 consecutive days. Remember, under Part B, the reimbursement is subject to only an 80-percent payment. The entire cost may be covered under Part A. Respite care is covered for up to 80 hours per year. In order to qualify, the following conditions must be met:

☐ The care must be for a chronically dependent individual. Medicare defines this as someone needing assistance with at least two activities of daily living (such as eating and bathing).

☐ The dependent person must have met either the catastrophic limit or the prescription drug deductible (discussed next).

☐ The care must be provided by a Medicare-certified home health agency.

The cost of Medicare

There are no premiums for Part A coverage. Enrollment in Part B is optional and there are monthly premium payments. The cost will increase every year; however, the increase cannot exceed the increase in anyone's monthly Social Security benefit. This prevents people from receiving smaller Social Security checks than those received in the previous year. In 1990, the monthly premium is about $36.

MEDIGAP

Medigap is supplementary insurance designed to pay for what Medicare does not cover. Despite Medicare's increased benefits, you will still be responsible for sizable deductibles, some co-payments, and other noncovered charges, especially in light of the low schedules of Medicare payments and the higher levels most doctors and hospitals charge.

Even ignoring long-term care costs, you could still face substantial out-of-pocket expenses for a host of other situations (for example, $560 initial hospital deductible, eight-day co-insurance for skilled nursing facility stays, payments after 150 days).

You want gaps covered, but you do not want to pay for some coverage twice. Put any Medigap coverage you consider under the fine print microscope to see exactly what it entails. Many of the same questions on the long-term health care policies checklist on pages 82–83 can be asked about a Medigap policy as well.

The bottom line: Medigap policies range from bare bones to blanket coverage. The key question is whether you can comfortably pay the difference between what Medicare covers and what you estimate you will owe. If you can, Medigap is not for you. But if you see yourself eventually facing, say, five-figure doctor bills, a policy covering 20 percent of the approved charges not picked up by Medicare could prove a life saver.

There are other instances when Medigap has less allure:

☐ If you are covered by a sound HMO or prepaid medical plan with competitive rates.

☐ If you are under a comprehensive company plan you can take with you into retirement.

☐ If your doctor accepts Medicare-assigned fees.

If you do want to explore the world of Medigap, here's a sample of what a major issuer, the American Association of Retired Persons (AARP), currently offers. Coverage changes rapidly. This information should serve only as a starting point. Also compare the policies issued by other established providers.

The most extensive AARP plan—Comprehensive Medicare Supplement—extends coverage for both parts A and B of Medicare as well as Medicaid and doctor care charges. Specifically it:

☐ Pays the actual in-hospital charges (per calendar year) up to the $560 deductible that you must pay before your Medicare benefits begin, plus 100 percent of the cost for the first three pints of blood.

☐ Pays (per calendar year) for 20 percent of Medicare-eligible expenses not paid by Medicare Part B after you pay the first $75 of such expenses, plus 100 percent of the difference between Medicare eligible expenses and usual and prevailing charges. Remember, eligible expenses are determined by Medicare. Your doctor may charge more.

☐ Pays you the following skilled nursing facility benefits (per calendar year): $25.50 Medicare co-payment for days 1 to 8; $140 each day for days 151 to 365.

☐ Pays you 80 percent of the usual and prevailing expenses for private duty nursing care when recommended by a physician, with no limit on the number of shifts covered.

☐ Pays you 50 percent of the usual and prevailing charges for prescription drugs that you buy while not confined in a hospital or skilled nursing facility after you pay the first $50 per calendar year ($500 a year limit).

The AARP also has what it calls a Recuperation Care Rider for an additional fee which includes:

☐ Benefits of $60 per day for up to 20 covered days in an eligible nursing home during any one calendar year.

☐ Benefits of $30 per visit for up to 40 covered visits by an RN, LPN, qualified therapist, or home health aide/homemaker during any one calendar year. Visits by a home health aide/homemaker must be a minimum of three hours per visit.

LONG-TERM HEALTH CARE (LTC)

Nobody plans to get sick or become an invalid or require nursing home services. But it happens. And if it does, a healthy retirement fund can be quickly depleted. It has been estimated that one year of nursing home care would financially destroy most elderly married couples as well as 90 percent of the elderly single.

Some people shrug and hope that government health programs, such as Medicare, will be sufficient. They are making a mistake. Others are depending on Medigap policies to get them over the hump. They're getting warm, but their security blanket is not so tightly wrapped as to give them ultimate protection.

Long-term health care refers to the services required to support an individual who is chronically ill or functionally handicapped. These services include a wide variety of medical, convalescent, or custodial care provided by physicians, nurses, home health aides, and others.

When you buy an LTC policy, you are protecting yourself against the possibility that you will require some extended care for chronic impairment when you get older. If you never need it, you are ahead of the game because you have been blessed with good health.

Long-term health care insurance policies cover extended stays in nursing homes or health-related facilities at either skilled, intermediate, or custodial levels, or sometimes home care in lieu of such confinement.

Putting a dollar sign on LTC policies

There is no such thing as a typical LTC policy. But here are some financial numbers to mull over before you get specific figures from a commercial insurance company or private group.

The price rises with age. For example, in one plan, the cost of a $120-a-day benefit over a six-year period, with minimum deductibles, is under $1,000 a year for someone who enrolls at age 60. The same policy costs over $3,000 at age 70 and close to $10,000 at 80. The lesson is buy young if you are going to buy.

Balanced against that is the cumulative cost of your policy premiums. If you pay $10,000 to $20,000 in premiums over the next 10 to 20 years, it may seriously affect your current standard of living. So an LTC policy might make less sense for someone in the low-income, low-asset (under $30,000) bracket. (The latter doesn't include your home, which is generally protected by law).

If you are in a higher bracket and your assets are more vulnerable, you must take the terms into account. Say you pay $600+ per year from age 55. That will cost you around $15,000 by the time you are 75 and likely to use it. If the policy terms give you $100 per day, you will quickly recoup that investment.

If you think you will have the assets to cover, say, 100 days of a nursing home stay, you can get coverage that lengthens the usual 20-day waiting period. Premiums will be much cheaper, by as much as a third. The longer the waiting period before coverage starts, the lower the premium.

Is long-term health care insurance a good buy?

Consider this scenario. You open an IRA at 40, invest $500 to start, and put in only $250 annually every year until you are 70½, the mandatory distribution age. Say you get 6½ percent compounded annually. The invested nest egg will be in the $26,000 range.

That may sound like a sizable amount, but consider this: The average cost of one year in a nursing home is between $20,000 and $40,000, and rising! Suppose you took that approximately $250 annual investment and bought an LTC policy. At the same age of 40, you might get coverage for up to $100 per day for skilled or custodial care for six years, with a 20-day waiting period. At a cost of between $7,000 and $8000 for that same 31-year IRA period, you would have a cushion that could be worth over $200,000!

What does an LTC policy buy besides care? Peace of mind; protection; less dependence on the goodwill of others to take care of you; more independence to make your own decisions and strategic moves; financial protection for your spouse; financial protection of your assets; and fewer headaches for those who might be called on (family and friends) to assist you in your time of need.

Shopping for the best LTC policy

The variations in policies, even within insurance companies, are numerous. Many options affect premium payments. Compare carefully and choose the best and most economical coverage for you. The dozen major variables and factors to be considered follow.

1. Daily benefit amount (amount to be paid for each day of covered claim). You choose, whether $20 per day, or $120. Do not take less than $80. Premiums are based directly on the benefit amount you elect. Check the daily charge for an intermediate care facility in your area today, and consider what inflation will do to that cost when, say, you hit 75.

Here's how an inflation rate of 5 percent a year would dramatically alter the average daily nursing home cost at a current base of $70.

Year	Daily charge
1990	$ 70.00
1993	81.03
1996	93.81
1999	108.59
2002	125.71
2005	145.54

2. The cost of the policy depends on the age at which you first buy it. Many policies are not available to people over 80. It is important to think about this kind of insurance early, especially if you are in good health now. Usually, the younger you are when you buy a policy, the lower the premium.

3. Generally speaking, you pay a relatively high premium for "first dollar" coverage in any form of insurance—that is, no deductibles, waiting periods, etc. Tip: Set aside a cash reserve on your own for that purpose. It is cheaper than paying the price of first dollar insurance coverage. Or consider insuring for about two-thirds of the amount of coverage you believe you will need. Some companies offer an inflation protection option that will automatically increase your daily benefit by a set percentage each year.

4. A policy that covers only skilled nursing care could be useless. Look for a policy that will cover you for intermediate and custodial care as well.

5. Some plans require that you first go the skilled care route before they pay for the biggest need, intermediate or custodial care. This type of plan may be cheaper, but it could also reduce your chances of receiving benefits.

6. Some policies require you to check into a hospital for three days before nursing home confinement is covered. This serves as a double check as to whether the nursing home care is medically necessary. Usually you must go into the nursing home within 30 days of your hospital confinement (some policies allow a bigger gap). A policy that does not have a pre-hospital requirement is definitely more flexible, but usually more expensive.

7. You will come upon policies that begin coverage on the day you enter a nursing home. Others require you to be confined a certain number of days (usually from 20 to 100) before your policy begins to pay. This is called a deductible period. Do not make the decision to take a long deductible because you think that Medicare will provide you with 150 days of coverage. The Medicare coverage only applies to Medicare-approved, skilled care facilities, and you may not qualify. However, the longer the waiting period, the lower the insurance premium cost, so if your financial resources can handle the first 100 days of care, the longer deductible is probably a wise choice.

8. Premiums are based on the cost of insuring people who are in normal good health when the policy is issued. If you have a preexisting condition—an illness or medical problem you have had within a certain period before you apply for a policy—and if it recurs within a certain period after you enroll, your claims can be denied. Most policies also have a contestable period, which may last up to two years, during which a company may challenge your coverage—even void it as of the issue date—if they can show you knew about an illness but didn't disclose it in your application.

9. Individual policies may be guaranteed renewable or optionally renewable. The latter can be canceled by a company on 30 days' notice. The former are renewed for life as long as you pay your premiums. That's what you want. Look for the renewable provision on the first page of your policy.

10. With a premium waiver, after you have been receiving benefits for a certain number of days (typically 90), you do not have to pay any more premiums until you are discharged. Some premium waivers refer to home health care as well.

11. You can keep the policy and review it for a specified time, usually from 10 to 30 days. If you are not satisfied, send it back and get your money back. Make sure the policy you are considering has this provision. Most states have laws requiring a "free look."

12. Most long-term health care policies do not pay for care related to nonorganic mental or nervous conditions, alcoholism, mental retardation, loss caused by war, or attempted suicide. However, you should look for a policy that does cover Alzheimer's disease, Parkinson's disease, senility, and other organic brain and nervous system disorders.

Questions about LTC insurance

When talking with your LTC policy salesperson, have this checklist of questions ready.

☐ How will benefits be paid? Does the plan reimburse for a given service at a fixed rate or pay a certain percentage of care costs? Is there a deductible period (also known as a waiting or elimination period)?

☐ What is the level of coverage? Is it defined as a daily maximum, a lifetime maximum, or some other way? What daily amount is paid for: skilled care, intermediate care, custodial care, home health care? How long (days, years) will you receive benefits for each? What is the most the policy will pay? Look for a policy that offers an $80-a-day benefit with a minimum of a three-year benefit period.

☐ What kinds of services are covered? Does the plan just cover nursing home stays, and if so, does it cover custodial and intermediate care as well as skilled? Does it cover services such as home health visits, adult day care, or respite care?

☐ Does the plan include an inflation escalator? (It definitely should.) Does it have options in deductibles, benefit amounts, length of confinement, so you can control what you get?

☐ What does the coverage you want cost? Per month, per year, for five years, ten years, a lifetime?

☐ Will the premium continue to be based on your age at enrollment? (You do not want one that rises with age.)

- [ ] If it is a company policy and you leave, can you convert coverage to an individual policy?
- [ ] How does A. M. Best Company rate the financial stability of this insurance company? (Look for at least an A- rating.)
- [ ] Will this policy pay even if you are covered by Medicare or Medigap?
- [ ] Does this policy contain any restrictive clauses like "not medically necessary" or "not reasonable or customary"?(If there is language you do not understand, have it explained.)
- [ ] How many home visits are allowed and what type of institution or home health organization may provide such services? Do such facilities exist in your area?
- [ ] Is there anything about the selling of the plan that hits you wrong? Too much hype? No personal contact with the agent? Is it an unrecognizable company with no proven customer service?

FLEXIBILITY IN PLANNING

Security comes at a cost, and sometimes that price can be pretty steep. But as you create your financial plan for retirement, it is important to factor in the health side of the equation. If you do not, your entire house of finances could crumble under one unexpected health setback.

SOURCES OF INFORMATION

Health care is a primary concern—physical, financial, and psychological—for everyone approaching retirement or planning for it. There are lots of sources of information. Here are just a few:

- [ ] Call (800) 888-1770 toll-free for answers to Catastrophic Act questions from the U.S. Department of Health and Human Services; also (800) 424-3676 for Supplemental Medicare Premiums from the Internal Revenue Service.
- [ ] Consumer Information Center (Department 529-T, Pueblo, CO 81009) for "Health Insurance for People with Medicare."
- [ ] American Council of Life Insurance (1001 Pennsylvania Avenue, N.W., Washington, DC 20004-2599) for "How to Use Private Insurance with Medicare."

- [ ] Call (800) 888-1998 toll-free for *The Medicare Handbook*.
- [ ] State insurance commissions and local Social Security Administration offices.
- [ ] United Seniors Health Corporation (1334 G Street, N.W., Suite 500, Washington, DC 20005).
- [ ] Health Insurance Association of America (P.O. Box 41455, Washington, DC 20018).
- [ ] Harold Evensky's *Planning for long-term health care*, also in the *Real life, real answers* series, is a complete guide to planning and choosing LTC options.

CHAPTER IX

Tapping the experts' and your own expertise

Y ou have probably heard the old saying that goes something like this: Who represents himself has a fool for a lawyer. The same holds true for certain aspects of your planning for a secure retirement, especially if you have a financially complex situation or a large estate.

The best advice is to get advice. Look to a coterie of experts—lawyers, tax accountants, real estate brokers, financial planners, insurance agents—to develop the best plan for your particular estate.

TAPPING EXPERTS' EXPERTISE

To select a financial planner, seek the advice of someone you respect, your lawyer or accountant, for example. You can get lists of financial planners in your area from The Institute of Certified Financial Planners (Suite 800, 2 Concourse Parkway, Atlanta, GA 30328) or Registry of Financial Planning Practitioners (2 Denver Highlands, 10065 E. Harvard Ave., Suite 320, Denver CO 80231). Once you have the names of at least three planners, first interview yourself, then interview them.

Ask yourself:

1. What are my financial goals? General and specific. Short- and long-term. Include all foreseeable factors surrounding retirement.
2. What is my personal investment philosophy? Establish parameters for risk and comfort, steady return, an eventual nest egg, and an investment mix.

3. How much personal involvement/control do I want?

4. What amounts are involved? What are my resources, expenses, budget?

Then ask your potential planners about credentials, sources of information, clients, a typical financial plan, and costs.

You can ask the same kind of questions of other types of money managers. Individuals who represent themselves as "investment advisers" should be asked if they are registered with the Securities Exchange Commission.

Bank trust departments, other than the trust officer in a large bank, are usually less sophisticated in retirement planning than are financial planners and stockbrokers. They are, however, major players in managing retirement funds, trusts, and estates.

TAKING ADVANTAGE OF YOUR TALENTS

One piece of advice those financial planners may offer is to consider some sort of additional post-retirement income through work. To get the ball rolling on post-retirement employment planning, ask yourself:

1. Do I have a marketable skill, or a plan to obtain one between now and retirement?

2. How much time do I want to spend working after I retire?

3. Do I have a hobby I could turn into a business?

4. What will interest me most in terms of combining a vocation with an avocation?

5. What is available today in the area in which I plan to live that may reflect available opportunities in the future?

Then, in an unhurried manner, start a program. Look at what others in your prospective position are doing today. Ask about the plans of colleagues and friends in similar situations. Keep an eye out for articles that open new vistas to explore. Network in your community. Try some volunteer associations that may open up for-profit opportunities for tomorrow.

If you have the time and inclination (and it is not against

company policy), try some moonlighting. Do the type of home work you envision doing when you retire.

WORKING AFTER RETIREMENT

Perhaps you have an adjunct business skill you could teach. Have you become proficient with computers? Would your involvement in company tax preparation translate into private practice? If you brought an old skill out of mothballs and polished it up, could it offer teaching possibilities?

The best way to explore whether teaching will satisfy you is to get your feet wet before you reach retirement. Check out local academic opportunities. Offer your services for night or weekend classes. See if you like it and then factor it into your retirement plans.

If you want to go a little beyond a hobby or teaching, consider a mini-business. With a hobby or mini-business, you can usually set your own hours and work at your own pace. Pulling in some discretionary income is all well and good, but there are some drawbacks. One is the tax man. Tight qualifications on what constitutes a business and what can be written off as a deduction can cause problems.

Then there's Social Security. As you saw in Chapter III, you begin to lose part of your Social Security check once you start to pull down serious dollars. For some, the extra effort just isn't worth the extra income when it's stacked against lost dollar benefits and time.

One route many executives take is some sort of consulting, especially with their former employer or another business contact. That way you do something you are good at and comfortable with, and the dislocation from the total work experience is less disruptive. But you are back in the work saddle again.

There is a lot to absorb and consider when you are planning for your retirement. But the key word is *planning*. Start early, revise your plans as conditions change, and stay flexible. Do that and your leisure years will be the best yet.

Real life, real answers.

The up-to-date library of personal financial information

How to make basic investment decisions
by Neal Ochsner

Planning for a financially secure retirement
by Jim Jenks and Brian Zevnik

How to borrow money and use credit
by Martin Weiss

How to pay for your child's college education
by Chuck Lawliss and Barry McCarty

Your will and estate planning
by Fred Tillman and Susan G. Parker

How to protect your family with insurance
by Virginia Applegarth

The easy family budget
by Jerald W. Mason

How to buy your first home
by Peter Jones

Planning for long-term health care
by Harold Evensky

Financial planning for the two-career family
by Candace E. Trunzo